BIRMINGHAM CINEMAS

THEIR FILMS and STARS 1900~1960

A NOSTALGIC JOURNEY

by

VICTOR J. PRICE

LET'S GO TO THE PICTURES

BREWIN BOOKS

First published in 1986 by
Brewin Books, Studley, Warwickshire.
Reprinted 1988
New Edition 1995
Reprinted August 1999

To Irene and Muriel, two friends who loved 'Going to the Pictures'.

God gave us memories so that we should have roses as Christmas.

The content of this book gives an historical account of the 125 cinemas
in Birmingham period 1900 – 1960 and includes 118 photographs
of buildings plus details of 5 new cinemas with photographs.

The moral right of the author has been asserted.

ISBN 1 85858 077 3

Typeset in Baskerville
and printed and made in Great Britain
by SupaPrint (Redditch) Ltd.

INTRODUCTION
by Alton Douglas

Somewhere inside my cranium there's an auditorium. Once ornate walls with peeling paint and rows of tip-up seats in need of an upholsterer's art facing deep red plush indefinite age curtains. Effortlessly I can dim the lights, signal the organ to sound a fanfare, swish open the drapes and flood the screen with magical light. My image and images of other auditoriums, other moments of settling down to enjoy nervousness and other veils revealing other worlds. Of course there are snatches of half remembered films too, but it's the picture palaces themselves that spark my senses.

I can go again to the Tivoli with its queues of ABC Minor Saturday morning kids fighting to be first in and out, clutch again Aunty Ivy's complimentary tickets for the Green Lane, given in return for a display card on the door of her outdoor in Cherrywood Road. I can still conjure up the Grange and Coronet where I first saw Errol Flynn and Wallace Beery, the Kingston where I fell hopelessly for June Allyson in "Little Women" — but above all I can recreate the Era. The Era was my cloud seven, my Valhalla, where I yelled at Johnny Mack Brown, Buster Crabbe and Gene Autry, my twenty foot heroes, and where I was once hit in the neck by an ice cream carton.

I can sometimes travel to the luxury of the Gaumont to see again that curious non-talkie "The Thief" starring Ray Milland, to the West End where I became hooked for ever on the music of Glen Miller or I can wander again amongst the fish tank splendour at the top of the Odeon steps.

Back again to the Ritz where my eight year old nephew, halfway through a particularly blood-thirsty western turned to me with fear filled eyes and said "Phew, I've finished with Injuns". But, as always, I drift back to my beloved Era, with its cases of stills, and its own peculiar smell. There my brother took his future wife on their first date, promising her, as a treat, the best seats in the house. She spent the whole evening in hysterics because there was no circle and the balcony was just one step high!

In my own way I've contributed, both as a viewer and as an artiste, in this television dominated age, to the demise of the cinema and of that I'm none too proud. However now, with the aid of Uncle Victor's splendid book, we can all once again be reminded of those far-off days and nights at the flicks.

Alton Douglas

FOREWORD

BIRMINGHAM CINEMAS 1900 – 1960 by Victor J. Price

Mr. Price, who is donating any royalties from this most interesting and informative publication to St Mary's Hospice, has given me the opportunity of explaining to readers the aims and aspirations of the Hospice.

St Mary's Hospice, now fully established and recognised as a "little branch of heaven" for the care of the terminally ill, especially those now suffering from cancer, needs increased support in order to continue to provide the much needed and invaluable service to patients in St Mary's Hospice and in their own homes in the Birmingham area, where patients are relieved from pain and the fear of pain.

We aim to provide total care — medical, nursing, spiritual and social, for all patients referred to us, either in the patients' own homes or in St Mary's, and no stone is left unturned in order to raise the standard of life of each individual patient to the highest possible level, whilst they are still with us. However, we need additional support to expand this work which we feel is so essential in the West Midlands, and also to provide a much needed Day Centre.

I would like to take this opportunity of recommending "Birmingham Cinemas 1900 – 1960" to you and also of congratulating Mr. Price on his initiative in having this book published.

J.M. Burke
Administrator — St Mary's Hospice.

CONTENTS

`To cure sometimes, to console often, to comfort always`

PREFACE

The first film show to be screened in this country was put on by the Lumiere Brothers, the French pioneers, on the 2nd February 1896 at the Regent Street Polytechnic in London. Since then millions of feet of celluloid have passed through projectors all over the world.

It was in Music Halls, Circuses and Fair Booths that film shows were first given and later in converted shops and public and church halls, then came the Picture Palaces or Houses and finally the Cinemas as we know them today.

The first, "Living Pictures", (as they were then called) it is claimed, were shown in the Aston area in 1888 by Pat Collins, the showman. It should be pointed out, however, that Aston was not absorbed into the Birmingham District until 1911.

Films were displayed on the screen at the Birmingham and Midland Institute in Paradise Street by the well known showman, Birt Acres, in 1897 — one film, was a realistic shot of a bull fight, this showed the bull rushing full tilt at the camera, the illusion was so complete that the audience was seized with momentary panic, and hurriedly vacated the first few rows of seats.

In addition to the two mentioned, in 1909, under the Cinematograph Act of 1909, the following establishments were licensed to exhibit moving pictures. This Act laid down strict official regulations for the exhibiting of film shows.

Co-operative Hall, Coventry Road, The Steam Clock, Morville Street, The Carlton Theatre, Saltley, The Palace Theatre, Bordesley, The Grand Theatre, Empire Theatre, Gaiety Theatre, King's Hall, Corporation Street, Curzon Hall, Suffolk Street, Digbeth Institute, Digbeth and Bingley Hall, King Alfred's Place.

Before the passing of this Act, one of the earliest establishments to show 'flickers', as they were then called, was a large shop in High Street, between New Street and the old Market Hall. There seated on boxes and other improvised seating, one could, for a copper or two, see trains entering or leaving stations, horses on exercise etc., afforded by a hand operated projector. This was a great novelty in those far off days and usually had a full house.

By far the most popular establishment for presenting moving pictures was the Curzon Hall in Suffolk Street, (the West End Cinema and Dance Hall was on this site), it was hired by the Midland Cinema veteran, Mr Waller Jeffs. This hall was originally built in 1865 as the home of the National Dog Show and other exhibitions and was a very popular place of entertainment. It eventually became a full time cinema.

I have also included in this book details of the films and the stars of the period, but, it is impossible to include all of them in a book of this nature. I hope that by reading it, it will bring back nostalgic memories to two generations of cinema-goers.

Victor J. Price.

Claudette Colbert

Gene Barry

SILENT FILMS

The most astonishing thing about the silent film era was its brief existence. In 1928 silent films had become sophisticated and accepted by all, as a medium capable of telling a story in a unique way. Within two years, this new art was almost dead, killed off by the synchronised talkies.

The years 1930–31, were the last completed years of the screen remaining silent in Birmingham. The main films shown being, "What Price Glory" with Edmund Lowe and Victor McLaglen, Adolphe Menjou in the film version of Marie Corelli's, "Sorrows of Satan". Emil Jannings and Phyllis Haver in, "The Way of all Flesh". Gloria Swanson in, "The Loves of Sunya". Ronald Colman, Vilma Banky and Gary Cooper in, "The Winnings of Barbara Worth". Emil Jannings and Camilla Horn in, "Faust". Rod La Rocque and Dolores Del Rio in Tolstoy's, "Resurrection". Janet Gaynor and Charles Farrell in, "Seventh Heaven", Rudoloph Valentino's last film, "The Son of the Sheik". Norma Talmadge in "The Dove", Charlie Chaplin in, "The Circus". Dolores Del Rio in, "Ramona". Gloria Swanson and Lionel Barrymore in "Sadie Thompson" and H.B. Warner and Hugh Williams in, "Sorrell and Son" from the novel by Warwick Deeping.

The most memorable and outstanding films this period produced included, "The Great Train Robbery" in 1903, it was a twelve minute long melodrama opening in a railroad telegraph office where bandits are forcing the operator to stop the approaching train. This film was hailed as an enormous success at that time. "Birth of a Nation" in 1915 with Henry B. Walthall and Lillian Gish, was an epic about the American Civil War and "Intolerance" in 1916 with Mae Marsh and Lillian Gish, employed some 20,000 extras and was, by far, the most expensive film made at that time. Both films directed by David Wark Griffith raised the cinema to the level of an art form. "The Ten Commandments" directed by Cecil de Mille in 1923, (second version was made in 1956) "The Covered Wagon" in 1923, "The Iron Horse" in 1924, the story of the expansion of the railroad bringing civilization and progress to the West. "The Phantom of the Opera" in 1926 (this was re-made in 1942 starring Claude Rains). "Ben Hur" in 1926 with Ramon Novarro. "The Dark Angel" in 1925 with Ronald Colman and Vilma Banky (this was re-made in 1935) "The Gold Rush" in 1925 with Charlie Chaplin. "The Big Parade" with John Gilbert and Renee Adoree a film about World War I. "The Thief of Bagdad" with Douglas Fairbanks in 1924. "Flesh and the Devil" in 1926 with Greta Garbo and John Gilbert a romantic melodrama. "The King of Kings" 1928 with H.B. Warner who was praised for his dignity in his portrayal of Christ. "Wings" 1927 with Clara Bow and Charles Rogers, the first motion picture to win an Academy Award., a film about the first World War. Other films nominated for this award were, "The Last Command"; "The Racket", "Seventh Heaven" and "The Way of All Flesh".

These films were shown at the popular rendezvous of the time, The West End and Futurist Cinemas. In the year 1929 you could pick and choose between silent and the new Talkie Films but by 1930 it was talkies all the way and the beginning of the golden era in the film industry.

In the 1920's over 900 films were distributed each year, throughout the United Kingdom.

Jackie Coogan was one of the first child stars, his first film was "Trouble" in 1922 and with Charlie Chaplin in "The Kid" in 1923.

Francis X. Bushman

Gloria Swanson

THE TALKIE ERA

The films that were shown had an influence on the mass audiences, and in effect, dictated their standards of behaviour, hair styles and dress. Mannerisms of the actor and actresses were copied and thereby the younger generation became better mannered and turned out, they took a pride in themselves which was not evident before. Mothers took the family to the 'Pictures', young men their girl friends, sometimes to win their favour. It became to millions a dream world and an appealing and exciting experience never to be forgotten. Going to the pictures became a way of life.

A.P. Herbert, the celebrated writer and politician wrote in 1929, "The talkie, was doomed to an early but expensive death", how wrong he was. In the 1930's the British Film Industry alone, turned out some 200 films a year, a large proportion of American films were imported into this country as well. In 1938 Birmingham had over 90 cinemas showing two performances each week, plus a Sunday performance.

I would like now to reflect upon some of the outstanding films of the period:—

"Blackmail", the first feature length British film, directed by Alfred Hitchcock, involving sound, this film will go down as a classic. The leading lady was a German actress, Annu Ondra, she spoke no English, so, he superimposed the voice of an English actress, Joan Barry. This was a new innovation or technique to be known as 'dubbing'.

"The Singing Fool", made in 1928 was the first full length talkie musical, starring Al Jolson, to be exhibited in Birmingham, songs from the film were, "Sitting on Top of the World", "The Spaniard that Blighted my Life" and "Sonny Boy". It broke all box office records when it was shown at the Futurist Cinema in Birmingham in March 1929.

"The Broadway Melody" made in 1929, with Anita Page, Bessie Love and Charles King. This was the first sound film to win an Academy Award. Musical numbers included, "You Were Meant for Me", "Broadway Melody" and "Give My Regards to Broadway".

"All Quiet on the Western Front" made in 1930 with Louis Wolheim, Lew Ayres and John Wray. The novel sold over 2 million 5 hundred thousand copies, second only to the Bible, when Universal Pictures purchased the film rights. It is destined to go down to posterity as a true and faithful record of the First World War. The film was banned in Germany for 20 years.

"Cimarron", made in 1931 with Richard Dix and Irene Dunne. The story was taken from the novel by Edna Ferber and is the story of the rise of Oklahoma from the early pioneer days of the statehood.

"Grand Hotel" made in 1932 with Greta Garbo, John and Lionel Barrymore, Joan Crawford and Wallace Beery. The entire setting for the film took place in a plush and glamourous Berlin Hotel.

"Cavalcade" made in 1933, with Diana Wynyard and Clive Brook. The film tells the story of a married couple's life period 1899 to 1932. It won three Adademy Awards.

"42nd Street" made in 1933 a classical musical with Warner Baxter, Ruby Keeler and Bebe Daniels.

"It Happened One Night" made in 1934 with Clark Gable and Claudette Colbert. It was one of the most refreshing of romantic screen comedies and won five Academy Awards.

"Mutiny On The Bounty" made in 1935 with Charles Laughton, Clark Gable and Franchot Tone, Laughton taking the part of the hateful Captain Bligh.

"The Great Ziegfeld" made in 1936 with William Powell taking the leading role and Myrna Loy and Frank Morgan. An epic film three hours long. It contained seven lavish production numbers.

"Gone With the Wind" made in 1939 with Clark Gable and Vivien Leigh, this film was voted the best film ever made by a panel of judges in 1984, a triumph for M.G.M.

"The Grapes of Wrath", made in 1940 with Henry Fonda and Jane Darwell.

"Rebecca" made in 1940 with Laurence Oliver and Joan Fontaine.

"Random Harvest" made in 1942 with Ronald Colman and Greer Garson.

"Dr. Jekyll and Mr. Hyde" made in 1941 with Spencer Tracy and Ingrid Bergman.

"Going My Way" and "The Bells of St. Mary's" made in 1944 with Bing Crosby.

"This Happy Breed" made in 1944 with John Mills and Celia Johnson.

"Brief Encounter" made in 1945 with Trevor Howard and Celia Johnson.

"The Glenn Miller Story" made in 1954 with James Stewart as Glenn.

"The Bridge on the River Kwai" made in 1957 with Alec Guinness and Jack Hawkins.

The "ROAD" films with Bing Crosby, Bob Hope and Dorothy Lamour 1940—1960.

The list is endless but I will conclude with mentioning some of the great films made in the 1930's:—

"The Sign of the Cross" with Charles Laughton as Neor.

"Queen Christina" with Greta Garbo and John Gilbert.

"King Kong" with Fay Wray, Robert Armstrong and Bruce Cabot.

"Scarface" with Paul Muni as Al Capone.

"The Farmer Takes a Wife" with Henry Fonda and Janet Garnor.

"Pygmalion" with Leslie Howard and Wendy Hiller.

"Sally in our Alley" made in 1931 and was one of 15 films made by Gracie Fields, she also made 500 records and gave 10 command performances.

The Tarzan adventure films with Johnny Weissmuller and Maureen O'Sullivan.

We certainly must not forget the cowboy heroes that gave us so much enjoyment, Tom Mix, Gene Autrey, William S. Hart, Harry Carey, Hoot Gibson, Ken Maynard, Buck Jones and Hopalong Cassidy. The comedy stars, Charlie Chaplin, Laurel and Hardy, Buster Keaton, Abbot and Costello, Harold Lloyd, Ben Turpin, W.C. Fields and Harry Langdon to name but a few.

We most certainly must not forget Elvis Presley, the Rock and Roll King, he made 32 films, the early ones being, "King Creole", "Jail House Rock" and "G.I. Blues". Cliff Richard will also be remembered for his films "Serious Charge" made in 1959 and "Expresso Bongo" in 1960.

My hope is that, by reading this book, you will feel all that nostalgia and that, you have indeed, been to the 'Pictures' once again.

DATUM:— The total seating capacity in all Birmingham Cinemas in 1938 was 117,000. In 1939 it had 98 cinemas, in 1950 - 86 and in 1960 - 45. There were thirteen organs installed in the Cinemas of Birmingnam.

Alfred Hitchcock the director with a genius for the horrific.

This photograph of film star Anna Neagle talking to Waller Jeffs, was taken in Birmingham in 1937. Herbert Wilcox, the film director who later married Miss Neagle, is in the background. Mr. Jeffs died in Stratford upon Avon in 1942.

CURZON HALL

Daily at 2-30 and 7-30.

THE WALLER JEFFS'
New Century Pictures and Entertainments.
AUTUMN SEASON NOW OPEN.

Curzon Hall,
THE HOME OF PICTURES.

MR. WALLER JEFFS' WINTER SEASON NOW OPEN
2.30.   TWICE DAILY.   7.30.

THE NEW CENTURY

PICTURES

SUPERB

LIFE-MOTION PHOTOS.

THE FESTIVAL OF THE SEASON,
THE BURGLAR'S BOY,
THE BABES IN THE WOOD,
THE PRINCE IN INDIA,
WINTER SPORTS,
THE TRAMP,
GRANDPAPA AND THE BUTTERFLY
'A TRIP UP THE NILE,
THE PYRAMIDS AND SPHYNX,
THE RISE & FALL OF NAPOLEON
VISIT TO THE CIRCUS,
STOLEN BY GIPSIES.

Launch of the "Dreadnought" by H.M. the King.

STATE OPENING OF PARLIAMENT.

MR. CUTHBERT ROSE.

Scottish Curlers at Kandestig.

Doors open 2.0 & 7.10   Early Doors at 6.45, Saturdays 6.30.

Popular Prices:—2/6, 1/6, 1/-, 6d., and 3d.

RESERVED SEATS AT HARRISONS.

MATINEES DAILY, EQUAL TO EVENING.

March 12th 1906

The CURZON HALL, situated at the top of Suffolk Street, Birmingham, was erected in 1864 as an exhibition hall and was the home of the National Dog Show. It was named after George Nathaniel Curzon, English statesman and the Viceroy of India 1899–1905.

Waller Jeffs, a showman of renown, first started showing animated pictures in this hall in 1899 and then living pictures which he billed as "Wonderful Illusions" in May 1901. During this year he gave over 200 performances. Prices of admission 3d in the gallery, 6d in the amphitheatre, 1/6 for boxes and 2/6 in reserved stalls. He also ran special shows for a combined tram and admission ticket for 1/—. It had a seating capacity of 3,000. It later opened as a full time cinema known as The New Century Picture Theatre. During the first World War it was used as a recruiting office. After extensive alterations it opened on the 9th March 1925 as the West End Cinema and Ballroom.

This building housed the first purpose built cinema in Birmingham, situated in Station Street, it opened on the 30th. July 1910 and was known as "The Electric Cinema", see full details of same under "Classic Cinema" on page 2.

The CLASSIC CINEMA, Station Street, Birmingham opened on the 30th July 1910, it was then known as "The Electric Cinema", proprietors Electric Theatres (1908) Ltd., a London based company. It was the first purpose built cinema erected in this city and is still operative today. In 1922 there was a change of ownership and it was re-named, "Select Cinema", it showed silent films until the end of May 1930, the last film being "Actress and the Angel" with Jack Mulhall and Greta Nissen. On Monday 2nd June it showed its first talkie, "Bulldog Drummond", with Ronald Colman. A poster erected outside invited people to "Come in and Listen". The manager at that time was Leslie Tonks. When it finally closed on the 14th November 1931 it was known as "The Select Repertory Cinema", films shown "The Living Corpse" and "Man with a Movie Camera". The building was used as an amusement arcade for some time afterwards but on the 20th March 1937, after extensive building alterations and re-furbishment it opened as Birmingham's second News Theatre, "The Tatler". Seating capacity 399, manager again being Leslie Tonks. In Jan. 1970 it became the "Jacey Cinema" and in 1980, "The Classic" opened as a two screen cinema under the management of James Debney. Seating No.1 – 242, No. 2 – 105. It was threatened with closure in September 1984 and was due to close on the 27th but, at the very last moment Brian Saunders, a cinema proprietor from Coventry, took out a 25 year lease and closure was avoided. He re-named it, "The Tivoli", the films chosen being, in No.1 – "Friday the 13th – The Final Chapter" (18) and in No.2 – "Insatiable" (18) and "Pick up Girls" (18).

Staff photograph of the staff at the 'Electric' was taken in 1911 when it was under the management of Geo. Putnam.

The GRAND THEATRE, Corporation Street, Birmingham (next door to the Kings Hall) opened as a cinema on the 1st September 1930, proprietors Universal Pictures Ltd., with the showing of the film, "All Quiet on the Western Front" with Louis Wolheim and Lew Ayres, this epic film also included in the cast Slim Summerville, John Wray, Russel Gleason and Beryl Mercer. It was directed by Lewis Milestone. It was only open as a cinema for a few years, it was then opened as The Grand Casino Ballroom and was a very popular rendezvous. It originally opened as a Theatre in 1883.

KINGS HALL PICTURE HOUSE, (next door to the Grand Theatre), Corporation Street, Birmingham opened in 1909 the proprietors and managers were J.P. Moore & B. Kennedy. It gave three performances daily. The photograph was taken from the Authorised Programme of the Royal visit to Birmingham on 7th July of that year for the opening of the Birmingham University. In 1912 it was known as the Royal Cinema De Luxe. In December 1914 it had a change of management and was re-named Corporation Street Picture House, this continued until 24th June 1918 when, again a change of name Kings Hall Picture House, the film shown was "Dick Carson Wins Through" with Henry Edwards and Chrissie White. It had a fine orchestra under the direction of Francis Drake, he was superseded by Norris Stanley. Closure finally came on Saturday 25th September 1920, film selected "The Market of Souls" with Dorothy Dalton.

The BULL RING CINEMA, situated in Park Street, off the Bull Ring and opposite St. Martin's Church, opened in 1863 as the London Museum Concert Hall, nicknamed "The Mucker", later it changed its name to The Canterbury Music Hall. It opened as a cinema in July 1912. In 1921 it was under the managment of P.J. Stokes. The film, "The Hunchback of Notre Dame" was shown in January 1929, with Lon Chaney taking the leading role. The admission charges then being 4d. It had a seating capacity of 480. It closed as a cinema in December 1931. The building is still standing today and operating as a Night Club and Karate centre.

Sol Levy, the Birmingham film magnate, bought the U.K. rights of this epic film in 1915 at a cost of £10,000 and grossed £100,000 a fabulous figure in those days.

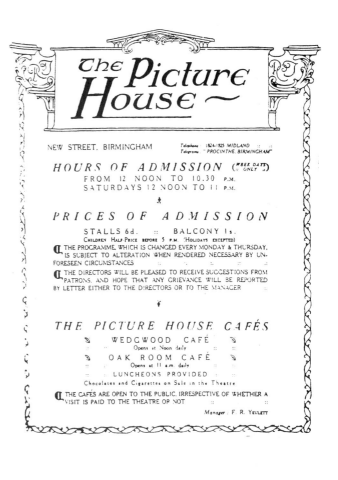

The PICTURE HOUSE, New Street, Birmingham was opened on the 20th October 1910 by Lady Noreen Bass the first performance was by invitation only. Prices of admission being 6d and 1/-. It was situated next door to the Theatre Royal. One of the earlier managers was C.J. Ling, in 1915 it was managed by F.R. Yeulett. The orchestra was under the direction of J. De Leeun. It was a favourite rendezvous and had two attractive cafes. It closed on the 5th June 1926 showing the film "Mike" with Sally O'Neill. The top facade of the original building is still intact today and can be seen as the entrance to Piccadilly Arcade. (below the interior).

Anne Crawford

Marilyn Maxwell

Jack Buchanan

The FUTURIST CINEMA, John Bright Street, Birmingham was built for Sol Levy and opened on the 30th July 1919 under the management of Charles Williams. It was one of the finest cinemas in the Country. Seating capacity 1,245. The opening films were "The Great Love" starring Lilian Gish and H.B. Waltham, the supporting film was "Our Little Wife". It was the first Birmingham Cinema to give a showing of a talkie film, "The Singing Fool", starring Al Jolson on the 18th March 1929, this broke all box office records, the manager at that time was Mr. Anthony. It closed in November 1940 owing to damage in an air raid on the City but re-opened on the 20th April 1943, the ceremony was attended by The Lord Mayor of Birmingham Councillor W.S. Lewis, J.P. and Group Captain J.A. Cecil Wright, M.P., the proceeds were given to charity, half to the R.A.F. Benevolent Fund and half to the Midlands Cinematograph Trade Benevolent Fund. The film chosen was "A Night to Remember", (an apt title) starring Loretta Young, Brian Aherne and Jeff Connell. On the 26th November 1981, after being closed for alterations, it re-opened as a two screen cinema, No. 1 seating 721 and No. 2 234. The film chosen being "Mommie Dearest" (AA) with Faye Dunsway, Monty Python's, "Life of Brian" (A) and "Airplane" (A). Proprietors Thorn/EMI Cinemas of London. The present manager is Peter McFadden.

Franklin Rangborn

The SCALA CINEMA, Smallbrook Street, Birmingham opened on the 4th March 1914 under the management of J.H. Graham Cutts. The film chosen was, "Confederates in Crime" a two part drama. It had a seating capacity of 800. Prices of admission 6d and 1/-. The proprietor was Sol Levy, a leading light in the trade at that time. In 1916 it was managed by Chas. Williams who later went to the Rookery Cinema. It was renowned for its orchestra which was under the direction of Handel Timperley. It was a real luxury cinema and one you went to on birthdays and holidays. It closed on the 4th June 1960 showing the films, "Teenage Lovers" (X) and "The Leech Woman" (X) the manager then being Derrick Cornford.

George Raft

Kirby Grant

The FORUM CINEMA, 88/90 New Street, Birmingham opened on the 1st November 1930 with the films, "Loose Ends" with Owen Nares and Edna Best and "Kiss Me Sergeant", with Leslie Fuller. Prices of admission Balcony 1/-, Stalls 1/3, Circle 2/- Grand Circle 3/-. It had a fine Compton Organ installed. It was originally called the Theatre de Luxe and was part of the Masonic Hall, it was owned by Electric Theatres (1908)Ltd and managed by A. Fletcher. In July 1910 it showed the films "State of Laos" "Sly Little Cupid" and "The Valuable Hat". It was later re-named The Regent and taken over by the A.B.C. circuit. Seating capacity 1,250. In May 1933 the management was taken over by E.B. Gold, known to his many friends as 'Manny', other managers were, Percy Freedman, Albert Harris, Lee Morgan, John Simmons and finally, when it closed on the 9th April 1983, Ian Brown, the film selected was "ET". (below the interior).

Griffith Jones

Ronald Colman

Kay Francis

The GAUMONT PALACE, Steelhouse Lane, Birmingham opened on the 19th February 1931, the film chosen for the gala performance was "Raffles", starring Ronald Colman and Kay Francis. The architect was William T. Benslyn, F.R.I.B.A. The manager was Leonard Putsman, he was superseded by J.P. Matthews in December 1944 and he by J. Alexandra in 1956. In 1938 43,000 people saw the Walt Disney film, "Snow White and the Seven Dwarfs". In 1963 it was converted for Cinerama and the number of seats reduced from 2,000 to 1,200. From 1965 to 1968 the film, "The Sound of Music" with Julie Andrews and Christopher Plummer was shown and, a Miss Jackson from Gravelly Hill North, Erdington, saw this film 130 times during this period. The last performance was given on the 29th October 1983 with the showing of the film, "Yellowbeard". It was demolished in August 1986.

Jack Evans, organist and under manager at the Gaumont Cinema period 1942–1946, sitting at the keyboard of the fine Compton Organ.

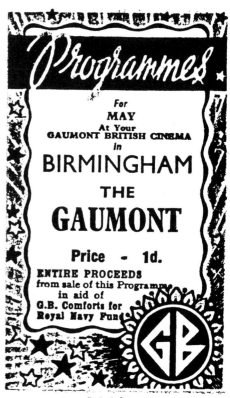

1944

Peter Finch

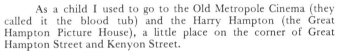

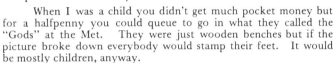

Susan Hayward

Sally Eilers

Conrad Veidt

The METROPOLE PICTURE PALACE, Snow Hill, Birmingham, known to the locals as 'The Met', opened in 1911 under the management of Joseph Levey.   Prices of admission 2d, 3d, 4d and 6d.   It had a seating capacity of 2,000.   In 1933 it was under the management of Wilfred J. Briggs.   It closed in 1941.   Prior to opening as a cinema it was a Theatre and Music Hall under the management of Walter Melville.

"I was born in Hampton Street, Birmingham at the bottom of Snow Hill.

As a child I used to go to the Old Metropole Cinema (they called it the blood tub) and the Harry Hampton (the Great Hampton Picture House), a little place on the corner of Great Hampton Street and Kenyon Street.

When I was a child you didn't get much pocket money but for a halfpenny you could queue to go in what they called the "Gods" at the Met.   They were just wooden benches but if the picture broke down everybody would stamp their feet.   It would be mostly children, anyway.

The following week we'd go to the Harry Hampton, which was a 1d (½d) to go in and you had a comic and a strip of caramel toffee for your penny.

Then, when I was 14, in 1929, we had the very first talking picture at the Metropole — Al Jolson in "The Singing Fool", my dad gave me sixpence for my birthday to go and see it.   I think that was the finest talking picture I have ever seen and when Jolson knelt on the stage and sang Sonny Boy I don't think there was a dry eye in the house."

Deborah Kerr

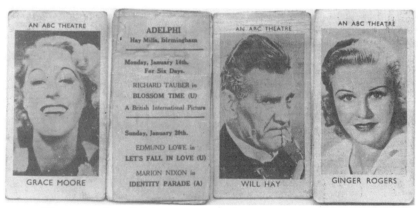

Chester Morris & Irene Hervey in the film The Three Godfathers 1949.

Mrs Doris Brown,
South Yardley, Birmingham.

Reginald Denny

Photographs of this type were given to patrons and were much in demand in the 1930's.

9

Richard Green

Janet Gaynor

The WEST END CINEMA, Suffolk Street, Birmingham was opened on the 9th March 1925 by Sir Whitworth Wallis. The feature film chosen was the great naval film, "Zeebrugge", this was followed by "Wanderer of the Wasteland" with Jack Holt. It had a fine orchestra under the direction of Harry Such. One of the early films shown was "The Squire of Long Hadley" starring Brian Aherne, the Birmingham film star. In 1926 J. Engleman became the musical director and in this year the cinema was acquired by Provincial Cinematograph Theatre Circuit, later to be absorbed by Gaumont-British and eventually by the Rank Organisation. On the 26th August 1929 it went over to sound showing the film, "Show Boat" starring Laura La Plante and Joseph Schildkraut., copies of this version of the film are now lost. The cinema had a fine restaurant and underneath was the West End Dance Hall a very popular rendezvous. On the 1st May 1933 the manager inserted an advertisement in the Birmingham Mail which read as follows:— "Egyptian Mummy required for hire, must be at least 3,000 years old". Mr George Cadbury saw the advertisement and was able to oblige as, some 30 years previous he had purchased a mummy of a Princess or high born woman of the 28th dynasty in the area of Pharaoh Neche and Pharaoh Hopkna who assisted King Zedekiah. The Mummy was exhibited to promote the film, "The Mummy", starring Boris Karloff, who, incidentally was an English actor real name William Pratt. The film was a great success. Many readers will remember the fine organ installed and played by Reginald Dixon. It was due to close on the 3rd April 1965 but was, at the last moment, given a two year extension by the council, it finally closed on the 18th March 1967 showing the films, "Return of the Seven" (A) with Yul Brynner, Robert Fuller and Julien Mateos, the supporting film was "Ambush Bay" (A) with Hugh O'Brien and Mickey Rooney. Managers J. Bowgen 1941–1946, W.L. Moneypenny 1946–1947, John Green 1948–1963, Graham Stringer 1963 to March 1967.

Phyllis Calvert

James Mason

John Barrymore

Margaret Lockwood

Alan Ladd

The NEWS THEATRE, 56 & 57 High Street, Birmingham (situated between New Meeting Street and Carrs Lane), sponsored by British Movitone News, was opened on the 18th January 1932 by Neville Chamberlain, Chancellor of the Exchequer and Alderman J.G. Burman, Lord Mayor of Birmingham. The premises had been re-built. "Round the World with British Movitone News" was the title of the entertainment. It consisted of some twenty items of news, with a special feature entitled, "See Birmingham First". "In this modern world of ours", said Mr Chamberlain in a pre-recorded film interview, "we have got so used to surprises that we have almost forgotten how to be surprised at all. I wonder what our grandfathers would have said if they had been invited to take their place in a theatre in the very middle of Birmingham and been told that, without leaving their seats they could see, not imaginary scenes, but real events and live persons taking part in these events in the most remote and distant parts of the world. No doubt they would have been very astonished. I can quite picture them saying to themselves, 'Why, this beats the old stories we used to read in the Arabian Nights of people being transported on a magic carpet to other countries and places!' "

It was the first Birmingham Cinema to have a moving illuminated display sign. It closed in March 1960, it was then owned by Jacey Cinemas Ltd. The site had previously housed: period 1910–1914, The Cinematograph Theatre, proprietors London & Provincial Theatres Ltd., 1918–1923, The Imperial Playhouse, 1923–1931, The Oxford Cinema, proprietors C & D Cinemas Ltd., later taken over by N. Cohen and Jacey Cinemas Ltd.

Robert Beatty

Bing Crosby

Bob Hope

The PREMIER

OF THE

PARAMOUNT THEATRE

BIRMINGHAM

September 4th, 1937

    The PARAMOUNT THEATRE, New Street, Birmingham opened on the 4th September 1937, the film chosen, "The Charge of the Light Brigade" starring Errol Flynn, Olivia de Havilland, Patrick Knowles and Nigel Bruce.   The General Manager was Leslie C. Holderness.   Seating capacity 2440.   The mammoth Compton Organ installed was played by Al Bollington. It became the ODEON in August 1942 and has remained a key Midland cinema in the Rank circuit. It closed in 1965 for major modernisation costing £70,000 which included The Warwick restaurant, with access from the circle lounge, seating 100 and was fully licensed. It re-opened on Thursday 25th June of that year with the showing of the provincial premier of Columbia's film, "Genghis Khan" starring Omar Sharif and James Mason, the showing was preceded by the stage appearance of Cliff Richard and The Shadows. The Lord Mayor of Birmingham, Alderman H.C. Taylor was present together with other civic dignitaries. Manager Leslie J. Harris. The present manager is Christopher Mott. Other managers Ted Hainge and Tony Harvey.

ONE OF THE SCREEN'S MOST VERSATILE STARS

James Cagney, who is regarded by many as one of the most versatile stars on the screen, heads the cast of the fast-moving musical production, "Something to Sing About," which comes to this theatre next week. The picture, which introduces a brilliant new discovery, Evelyn Daw, presents Cagney as a New York orchestra leader who is signed to a film contract, taken to Hollywood and there transformed into a star.

"SOMETHING TO SING ABOUT"—HERE JUNE 12th WEEK

Mary Pickford

Warner Baxter

Lewis Stone

PERSONAL APPEARANCE OF GEORGE FORMBY
ON THE STAGE AT THE PARAMOUNT MARCH 28th WEEK

Dorothy Wilson

FUTURIST
THE HOME OF REAL ENTERTAINMENT
PRESENTS
THE FINEST AND BEST SHOW IN TOWN!
CAROLE LOMBARD
FRED McMURRAY
The Most Romantic Sweethearts of the Screen.
IN
HANDS ACROSS THE TABLE — (A).
A Paramount Picture.
WITH
ASTRID ALLWYN, RALPH BELLAMY.
SHE WANTED A MILLIONAIRE. HE WANTED
AN HEIRESS. BUT WHO WERE THEY TO
ARGUE AGAINST LOVE!
ADDED
THRILLING, EXCITING, SPY DRAMA!
WYNNE GIBSON,
FRITZ KORTNER,
IN
"THE CROUCHING BEAST" — (A).
From the famous "Clubfoot" Novel by Valentine Williams.
WITH
RICHARD BIRD, ANDREWS ENGLMAN.
ISOBEL JEANS, FRED CONYNGHAM.
THRILLING, TERRIFYING.
ALSO
"HOLLYWOOD EXTRA GIRL."

THE GAUMONT PALACE
TO-DAY FROM 12 NOON
The Next Wonder of the World.
"THE TUNNEL" — (U).
WITH RICHARD DIX, MADGE EVANS,
LESLIE BANKS, HELEN VINSON,
And Special Portrayals by
GEORGE ARLISS and WALTER HUSTON.
At 1.30 3.20 6.10 & 9.10.
In Addition Regis Toomey in "BARS OF HATE" (A)
GAUMONT BRITISH NEWS.

SCALA
TO-DAY,
SHIRLEY TEMPLE,
JOHN BOLES
IN
"CURLY TOP" — (U).
JAMES DUNN,   ALSO   IN ARLINE JUDGE
"WELCOME HOME" — (U)
BARGAIN HOURS: 12.30 to 4.30.
CAR PARK ADJOINING THEATRE FREE TO
PATRONS
Sunday Next: "THE DARK ANGEL" — (A).

WEST END CINEMA.
A GAUMONT BRITISH THEATRE.
TO-DAY AT 12.44, 3.30, 6.16, 9.2.
EDMUND GWENN,
LUCILE WATSON IN
"THE BISHOP'S MISADVENTURES" — (U)
Also LEW AYRES, MAE CLARK in "SILK HAT KID" (U)
AND BRITISH MOVIETONE NEWS.

WEST END DANCE HALL.
DANCING TO-DAY, 3 to 6 .... Admission 9d.
TO-NIGHT 8 to 11 .... Admission 1.6.
AL BERLIN AND HIS BAND.
THE SUPERIOR HALL FOR CLUB DANCES.

Carole Lombard

Shirley Temple

Continuous from 12.30 to 10.45. THE FORUM. Telephone: MID. 4519.
BORIS KARLOFF,
MARIAN MARSH, ROBERT ALLEN
IN
"THE BLACK ROOM" — (A).
To Love Him was to Vanish . . . Forever!
VIRGINIA BRUCE, DONALD COOK,
TED LEWIS and his ORCHESTRA,
IN
"HERE COMES THE BAND" — (U).
Happiness, Harmony and Hilarity.
NEXT WEEK: The Picture of 1936, CLAUDETTE
COLBERT in "SHE MARRIED HER BOSS" (U).

THE NEWS THEATRE, HIGH ST
Cont. 12.30—11.0.   6d. and 1/-
PRESENTS
THE LATEST NEWS, SPORT AND TRAVEL,
INCLUDING
THE KING'S VISIT TO CLYDEBANK.
BRITAIN'S WONDER SHIP,
"THE QUEEN MARY."
THE NEW ZEPPELIN LZ 129
LEAVES ON TEST FLIGHT.
AND
A WALT DISNEY COLOURED SILLY SYMPHONY.
"MUSIC LAND."

Boris Karloff

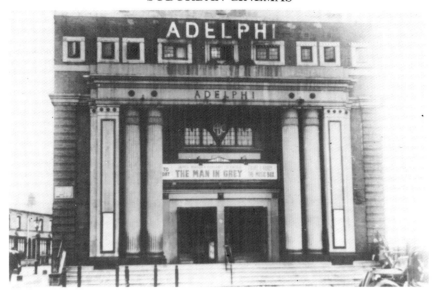

The ADELPHI SUPER CINEMA, Coventry Road, Hay Mills, Birmingham was opened on the 10th October 1927 by Councillor G.P. MacDonald, J.P., the films chosen were, "Diplomacy" with Blanche Sweet and, "Man Bait" with Marie Prevost and Douglas Fairbanks Jnr. It was erected adjacent to the site of the old Hay Mills & Yardley Picture House which opened in May 1913. It had a seating capacity of 1,234. Prices of admission 6d, 8d, 1/- and 1/3. The manager was J. Windsor Stevenson. The orchestra was under the direction of Carl Bent. In 1943 it was managed by Alex. Seymour and in 1965 by H. Frank Crane. Proprietors A.B.C. circuit. In 1941 the cinema presented the documentary film, "Target for Tonight" this was directed by Harry Watts for the Crown Film Unit. A 'Spitfire' Fighter was put on display on the forecourt to promote the film which had no professional actors only personnel in the R.A.F. When the film "The Last Coupon" (made in 1932) was shown the enterprising manager, transformed the cinema car park into a football pitch complete with goal posts and had it floodlit, to promote the film which was a comedy about a pools winner. It closed on the 31st August 1968 showing the films, "Blue" (A) with Terence Stamp and Joanna Pettet and "Rogue's Gallery" (A) with Roger Smith.

The ALBION PICTURE PALACE, 46a Holyhead Road, Handsworth, Birmingham, opened on Thursday 16th December 1915 by Councillor John White. Manager Harry Calver. Architect Horace G. Bradley. The film chosen was "Salambo" a World Masterpiece in Kinematography. Doors opened at 6.40 p.m. and the programme was continuous until 10.30 p.m. Prices of admission, 3d, 4d, 6d, & 9d. Seating for 800 but it had a waiting capacity for 300 patrons which was under cover. It was enlarged

in the 1940's and CinemaScope installed, seating extended to seat 1,000. In 1957 prices of admission ranged from 1/- to 2/3, the manageress was then Miss Winifred Smallwood. It closed on Saturday 24th September 1960, the films chosen, "The Mountain Road" (U) with James Stewart and Lisa Lu and "Death of a Princess" (A). (The interior was luxurious as can be seen in the opposite photograph).

This is a typical Quad Crown Poster that was displayed at the majority of cinemas.

Typical Uniform of an ABC doorman and usherette of the period. Remember the Black Cat, Army Club and De Reske cigarettes she used to sell?

The ALHAMBRA CINEMA, Moseley Road, Birmingham opened on the 26th December 1928, the opening ceremony was performed by Jameson Thomas, the British Screen artist and supported by the Lord Mayor of Birmingham S.E.M. Stephens and Leon Salberg. The film chosen for this grand opening was "The Scarlet Pimpernel" with Matheson Lang playing the principal role. It had a seating capacity of 1,261. The manager was L.H. Elbourne. It was built on or near the site of the 18th century Moseley Theatre which was erected about the year 1777. It closed on 31st August 1968 when it was known as the Moseley ABC, the film chosen was "The Fall of the Roman Empire" (U) an apt title, starring Sophia Loren and Stephen Boyd.

The original Alhambra was a palace of the Moorish kings in Granada in Spain, this cinema was built on a design to symbolise it. A special feature was the auditorium ceiling light which consisted of a six foot diameter glass bowl, representing the sun, set in an azure Mediterranean sky. The ceiling was beautifully finished and lighted by means of reflectors artfully concealed in special troughs, behind the striking Moorish tile cornices, which helped, to create the illusion of an outdoor setting.

Clark Gable

Anna Neagle, C.B.E.
1904 - 1986

16

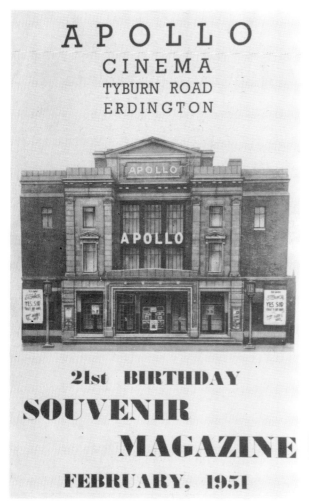

APOLLO
CINEMA
TYBURN ROAD
ERDINGTON

APOLLO

21st BIRTHDAY
SOUVENIR
MAGAZINE
FEBRUARY, 1951

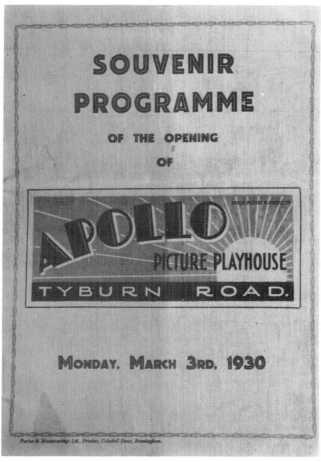

SOUVENIR
PROGRAMME
OF THE OPENING
OF

APOLLO PICTURE PLAYHOUSE TYBURN ROAD.

MONDAY, MARCH 3RD, 1930

THE BALCONY ENTRANCE

A CORNER OF THE VESTIBULE

The APOLLO PICTURE PLAYHOUSE, Tyburn Road, Erdington, Birmingham, opened on the 3rd March 1930, the film chosen was a musical comedy, "Follies of 1929" starring John Breeden and Sharon Lynn. The manager was Ernest Ellerslie. Every patron was presented with a mounted farthing, with the wording, 'Good Luck keep me and you will never be broke'. The second manager was Capt. Harry Thorburn, D.F.C., M.C., and he was followed by W.H. Fletcher, before being appointed to this position he played the Compton Organ that was installed in this fine cinema. It was the first cinema in Birmingham to have Hollophane Lighting installed. It had a seating capacity of 1,230. It closed on Saturday 1st April 1960 showing the films, "Last Train from Gun Hill" (A) starring Kirk Douglas and Anthony Quinn and "High Hell" (A).

The ASHTED ROW PICTURE HOUSE, Ashted Row, Birmingham opened on Thursday 5th December 1912 under the management of William Devey, the director was John Devey. It advertised Brilliant Opening Performances, prices of admission 2d, 3d, 4d and 6d. Seating capacity 1,000. In 1934 it was refurbished and opened as The New Ashted Row Picture House, in the 1940's it was under the management of A.N. Ardagh. It closed in 1958.

Aston Cross Picture House

Proprietors—The Aston Cross Picture House Ltd.
Manager—H. S. Perfect.

WEEK'S PROGRAMME

MON., TUES., WED., AUGUUT 13, 14, 15

1. SCENIC JAPAN (Interest).

2. A STRANGE ADVENTURE
A Deligntful and Clever Comedy, Featuring Jack Pickford and Bessie Byton. Two Famous and Popular Stars.

3. THE PURPLE DOMINO
Episode 12—"THE VAULT OF MYSTERY."

4. THE THREE GODFATHERS In Five Parts
A Fascinating Story showing how rough men can play the part of the Good Samaritan. Featuring Harry Carey and Stella Razetto.

TWICE NIGHTLY—Mon. & Sat. at 6-45 and 8-45. Conti

SPECIAL MATINEES—Mon. and Wed. at 3 o

Prices of Admission: Lounge 7d. (Booked for 3d extra).

—Phone: East. 430.

The ASTON CROSS PICTURE HOUSE, Lichfield Road, Aston, Birmingham opened in May 1913. Prices of admission 3d and 6d. Seating capacity 900. In 1915 it was under the management of Harry Trevanion. It was a popular rendezvous for Astonians. It was taken over by the ABC circuit in the 1950's and known as the A.B.C. Aston. It closed on Saturday 23rd August 1969, films chosen, "Tarzan and the Jungle Boy" (U) and "Gentle Giant"(U).

Frances Gifford

18

The drawing was made shortly after the building was opened as the 'Theatre Royal' in 1893.

The ASTORIA CINEMA, Aston Road North, Birmingham. On the 23rd September 1892 an agreement was signed, between George and Robert Hall to erect a theatre on this site to be called The Theatre Royal, Aston, this was duly built and opened. On the 12th December 1927 it opened as a cinema with a seating capacity of 1,194. The films chosen were The British Legion Film, "Remembrance" with Capt. Rex. Davis, M.C., Enid Stamp and Alf Goddard. A Miss Mary Wynn, a professional singer, was engaged to sing during this moving film. The other film was, "The Fighting Stallion" with Yalima Canutt. On the 26th November 1955 it gave its last performance with the film, "The Dambusters", with Michael Redgrave, Richard Todd, Basil Sydney and Patrick Barr playing the principle roles.

An unusual feature of this cinema was that it had rear projection, the projectors being situated 25 feet behind the screen. After closure it was converted into a T.V. Studio, the first performance was screened on the 17th February 1956. In 1974 it was taken over by BRMB Radio Station.

Betty Grable

The ASTON PICTURE PALACE THEATRE, 1 Lozells Road, Aston, Birmingham, opened on the 9th July 1910 at 4.00 p.m. by his Worship the Mayor of Aston, Alderman A. Taylor, J.P. The Manager was Frederick Jeffrey, he was superseded by Horace P. Tucker. Aston was, at that time a separate Borough of Birmingham. It had a short life and closed in 1915.

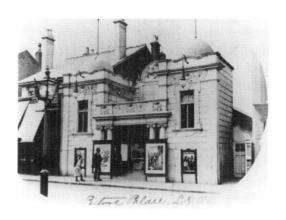

The ATLAS CINEMA Flaxley Road, Stechford, Birmingham (by night) opened on the 6th March 1938 the ceremony was performed by Sir John Smedley Crooke, M.P. The film selected was "Cavalcade" starring Fiona Wynyard and Clive Brook. It had a seating capacity of 1,348. The architect was E.S. Roberts, L.R.I.B.A. When it closed on the 30th May 1959 it was under the management of L.A. Gibbons, films chosen were "Room at the Top" (X) with Laurence Harvey, Simone Signoret and Donald Wolfit, the 'B' film was "Mail Van Murder"(A).

The BALSALL HEATH PICTURE HOUSE, Balsall Heath Road, Birmingham opened in November 1913 under the management of Alfred Edward Elborne, proprietors Balsall Heath Picturedrome Ltd. Prices of admission floor 3d and 4d, Grand Lounge 6d. It had a High Class Orchestra. Seating capacity 650. In 1920 the manageress was Lilly Pearl. In the 1940's it was re-named "LUXOR". It was an Asian cinema for a number of years before it finally closed in 1983.

The BEACON CINEMA, corner of Birmingham and Queslett Road, Great Barr, Birmingham was opened on the 7th March 1938 by Councillor Clifford Rowley, chairman of the Highways Committee Aldridge District Council, also present was Captain S.W. Clift, chairman of the Board of Directors. The film chosen was "Oh Mister Porter" (U) with the comedian actor Will Hay. It had a seating capacity of 1,200, the architect was R. Satchwell L.R.I.B.A. It closed on the 16th December 1972, showing the films, "The Nympho" (X) and "Erotic Three".

The BAKER STREET PICTURE HALL, Baker Street, Handsworth, Birmingham, when it opened in 1910 it was known as The Handsworth Picture Hall. Prices of admission ranged from 3d to 9d. It was Licensed for Music. Seating capacity 500. In 1913 the managing director was Joseph Dodd. In 1915 it was managed by G.E. Tillotson. It closed in the early 1920's.

Charles Boyer

The BEAUFORT CINEMA, Coleshill Road, Washwood Heath, Birmingham opened on the 4th August 1929 by Colonel H.J. Hutt, D.S.O., J.P. supported by Jameson Thomas the British Film Star. The film chosen was "The Scarlet Pimpernel", music was provided by the Sam Mey's Orchestra and the mighty compton organ installed, played by Eric Spruce. It had a seating capacity of 1,200. Prices of admission ranged from 6d. to 1s. It closed for renovation and enlargement in 1937 and was re-opened on Sunday 18th September of that year with an added seating capacity of 500. The films chosen were "The Case against Mrs Ames" with Madeleine Carroll and George Brent, and "Border Flight". The manager appointed was Freddie Studd. It became a venue for organ enthusiasts and became famous on the radio for recitals by Reginald New. It finally closed on the 19th August 1978 showing the films, "Warlords of Atlantis" (A) with Doug. McClure and Peter Gilmore and "Watch out we're Mad"(A).

Birchfield Picturedrome, Perry Barr

April 1914

Secretary · · · · · · W. J. S. Green.

Monday, Tuesday & Wednesday, 6th, 7th, & 8th,
The Bull Fighters of Spain, a Special Film. The Diver, Vitagraph Drama.
Thursday & Saturday, 9th, & 11th,
The Judgment of the Jungle, Drama. The Twentieth Century Farmer, Drama.

For Friday 10th, we are opening with a special programme for that day only.

Matinee, Monday & Wednesday at 3 o'clock. Saturday continuous from 3 to 10-30.

Prices—**Body of Hall, 3d. & 6d.; Grand Balcony, 9d.**
CHILDREN 2d., 3d. & 5d.

The BIRCHFIELD PICTUREDROME, Birchfield Road, Perry Barr, Birmingham, opened on Thursday 16th October 1913 film chosen, "Mimisa San" a stirring Japanese Drama with Madame Saharet in the title role, other high class films were also shown. Prices of admission, Body of Hall 3d & 6d, Grand Balcony 9d. Manager E. Johnstone he was superseded in 1914 by S. Lawrence. Seating capacity 900. It was built on the site of the old Perry Barr Police Station. Builders T. Elvin & Sons, Architect Scott & Weedon. It was one of the first suburban cinemas to have CineScope installed. It closed on the 3rd March 1962 showing the film, "South Pacific" with Mitzi Gaynor and Rossano Brazzi whose voiced was dubbed by Ezio Pinna the opera singer.

The BORDESLEY PALACE CINEMA, situated on the corner of Clyde and High Street, Bordesley, Birmingham 12. It was originally a theatre of renown, opened as a cinema in 1929 with a seating capacity of 1,296. The proprietors being Associated British Cinemas Ltd. The manager in 1936 was H. Walker, it had a succession of managers but when it closed in 1942 it was under the management of Miss M.C. Cooper.

THE BORDESLEY

PALACE

PROGRAMME FOR
NOVEMBER 1939

Manager Mr. Jim Marshall

Telephone: MIDland 0022

Kathryn Grayson

George Brent

Marsha Hunt

BOURNBROOK

ELECTRIC THEATRE,
Grange Road, Bournbrook.

Proprietors · Bournbrook & Selly Oak Electric Theatre Co.
Managing Director · · A. A. JAMES (A.I.Mech. E.)
Resident Manager · · · · F. V. JAMES

7-0 TWICE NIGHTLY 9-0

Matinees — Monday, Wednesday & Saturday at 3 p.m.

Only the best and latest Pictures shown

'Romance of the 60's." A Thrilling War Drama.

" The Fighting Schoolmaster," A Vitagraph
Drama.

Popular Prices, 3d., 6d. & 1/-

The BOURNBROOK ELECTRIC THEATRE, Grange Road, Bournbrook, Birmingham. Opened on the 13th November 1911 by A.C. Hayes, Esq., J.P. and C.C., it was advertised as 'Palatial' Seating capacity 620. The advertisement displayed was inserted in the local press in January 1912. It closed in September 1933 and the premises were taken over by the Ariel Motor Co.

Grace Kelly

Gene Kelly

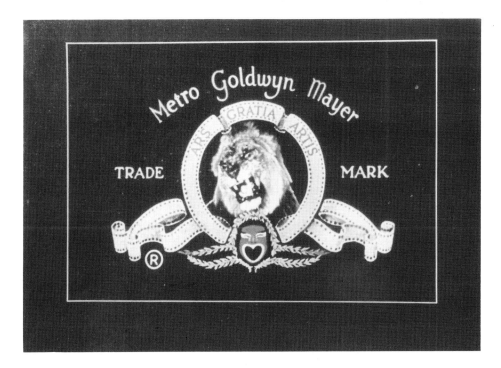

One of the best known lions in the film business is LEO, the big Nubian lion depicted in the M.G.M. trade mark and shown in front of every picture they produced. It was a roaring success!

Bristol Street
PICTURE HOUSE

Proprietors - - Edgbaston Picture Palaces, Ltd.
Managing Director - - Mr. J P. Moore

Matinees Daily at 3.

(COOL and COSY)

EVENING CONTINUOUS 6-30 to 10-45.

Enormous Success of 6 Changes
ALL BEST PICTURES.

GIGANTIC PROGRAMME
WEEK of JULY 13th, 1914.

MONDAY,
HIS GUILTY CONSCIENCE

The Mystery of the Talking Wire :: The Rich Man's Redemption
The Kidnapped Pugilist :: His Reputation at Stake
A Strenuous Ride.

TUESDAY,
In the Moon's Rays
The Miracle of Love :: The Death Warrant :: A Thief Catcher

WEDNESDAY,
INTO THE WILDERNESS
THE FRIENDLESS REDSKIN :: THE BULLY'S DOOM
The Way to Heaven :: The Lackey :: Polidor Wins a Bride

THURSDAY,
The AFGHAN RAIDERS
Thousand Dollars Reward :: The Silver Loving Cup :: A Man's
Faith :: Kids' Auto Races

FRIDAY,
LOVE'S CRUELTY
Madcap Jeanette :: The Governor's Double :: Mike and
Jake for Matrimony.

SATURDAY,
THE BLUE HEART
In Amalfi :: Peter's Evil Spirit :: The Midnight Call
The Guest of the Evening :: She was a Peach

Two Children's Matinees every Saturday at 2 and
3-30. 1d., 2d. and 3d.
The Early Matinee on Saturday includes Special Indian and Travel
Pictures.

Seats Booked in Advance. Plan at Pay Box

NO ADVANCE IN PRICES :
1s., 6d., 3d., And a Small Number 2d.

Wones, Typ., West Bromwich. B'ham Office—36 Cannon St.

The BROADWAY CINEMA, situated on the corner of Wrentham and Bristol Street, Birmingham. When it opened originally as a cinema, it was known as The Electric Picture House, later changing its name to Bristol Street Picture House (see display notice for details). In 1923 the property was demolished and re-built and opened on the 2nd April of that year as "The Broadway", under the management of Bernard F. Smith, the film chosen was, "The Storm" with House Peters. Prices of admission 6d, 9d & 1/3. It had a fine orchestra under the direction of Emile Van Loo. In later years it was directed by Noel Wimperis who, in 1929, moved to the Warwick Cinema, Acocks Green. On the 9th March 1931 it went over to 'talkies' showing the film, "Love Parade" with Maurice Chevalier, Jeanette MacDonald and Lupino Lane. On the 26th April 1956, after undergoing considerable alteration, it was opened by the Lord Mayor of Birmingham as "The Cinephone" specialising in foreign and sex films, this closed on the 17th September 1977 showing the films "Seduction" (X) and "Swedish Playgirls" (X). It was later re-named "Gala Cinema" and finally "Climax Cinema", this being a private cinema for members only, this closed in 1984.

The BRISTOL CINEMA, Bristol Road, Edgbaston, Birmingham, opened on Sunday 16th May 1937, the ceremony was performed by F.J.L. Hickinbotham, Esq., J.P. The feature film was "Luckiest Girl in the World", with Jane Wyatt, Louis Hayward and Eugene Pallette, the supporting film was "Land Without Music", with Richard Tauber, Diana Napier, June Clyde and Jimmy Durant. It had a seating capacity of 1,710. In 1943 the General Manager was Alfred G. May. On the 26th July 1972, after being closed for extensive alterations, it opened as a three screen cinema, No. 1 has a seating capacity of 482, No. 2 – 353 and No. 3 – 175. The three films chosen were "Henry VIII and his Six Wives" (A) with Keith Michell playing the principle role, "I am a Dancer" (U) with Rudolf Nureyev and the "Mutiny on the Buses" (A) with Reg Varney. The present manager is H.W. Price, the proprietors Thorn/EMI Cinema Ltd., of London. It closed on 24th. September 1987 and the building was demolished a few weeks later.

John Mills

Merle Oberon

David Niven

Michael Rennie

The CAPITOL CINEMA, Alum Rock Road, Birmingham was opened on Easter Monday 13th April 1925, the film chosen was "Sporting Life" with Reginald Denny. Prices of admission 6d, 8d & 1/-. It had a first class orchestra. In 1929 it was enlarged, seating capacity being Balcony 378, auditorium 1029. In 1957 the manager and licensee was William Moseley. In 1979 it was converted into a three screen cinema, seating capacity No. 1 –325, No. 2 –259 and No. 3 – 130. The present manager is Michael D. Blackmore and the proprietors Capitol Cinema (Ward End) Ltd. The Cinema is reputed to be haunted by two ex-patrons, a grey haired gent and a lady.

One of the most famous posters in the film industry relating to the film 'The JAZZ SINGER' made in 1927. Al Jolson's remark, in this film, "Wait a minute, wait a minute, You Aint't heard nothin' yet" — is now world famous.

The CARLTON CINEMA, Taunton Road, Balsall Heath, Birmingham opened on Whit Monday 28th May 1928, the film chosen being "Brigadier Gerard" by Conan Doyle, the principal part was played by Rod la Rocque. Muscial entertainment was provided by the Distingu Orchestra. Seating capacity 1,500. Proprietors M.W.T. Ltd., who were also the proprietors of the Coliseum Picture House, Saltley, previously known as The Carlton Theatre, Manager A.S. Cooke. On the 25th October 1940, during the showing of the film "Typhoon" starring Dorothy Lamour and Robert Preston, it was bombed during an enemy air raid on the City, several patrons being killed. Prices of admission then being Balcony 1/- & 1/3. Auditorium 6d & 9d. It was the first cinema in the City to have a lift installed for its patrons. It was later taken over, after repair, by Albert William Rogers a well known gentleman in the cinema world in Birmingham and re-opened on the 18th December 1943 with the showing of the film "The Rains Came" (A) with Myrna Loy, George Brent and Tyrone Power. In 1958 the General Manager was A.G. May. It ceased to operate as a cinema in October 1980 showing mainly Asian films under the management of K.K. Maini. Several licenses for Public Entertainment in the form of Music and dancing on the premises were issued between February and August 1983 when the proprietors were Mr. J.R. Hoo and Mrs Norma Thorpe. The premises after this period closed and became derelict and demolished in December 1985.

CASTLE
CINEMA

CASTLE BROMWICH

RESTAURANT
and
MILK BAR

Lets go to the
Pictures

The CASTLE CINEMA, Chester Road, (corner of Timberley Lane) Castle Bromwich, by night. Opened on Saturday 31st August 1940 with the films, "Out West With The Hardy's" (U) one of the favourite Hardy Family Films with Lewis Stone, as Judge Hardy and Mickey Rooney, the 'B' film was "The Magician's Daughter". It was owned by Harry Dare and the architect was Ernest S. Roberts. The interior of the cinema was lavishly decorated in Tudor Style. When it closed on Saturday 26th May 1963, showing the films, "Splendour in the Grass" (X) with Natalie Wood and Warren Beatty, it was under the management of W. Wakefield. The 'B' supporting film was "Return of a Stranger" (A). The building was later demolished.

One of the series of Drummond films
made in the 1930's.

The CLIFTON CINEMA, Walsall Road, (corner of Tower Hill), Great Barr, Birmingham opened on the 21st February 1938 with the films, "The Devil is Driving" (A) with Richard Dix and "Talking Feet" (U) with Hazel Ascot. It had a seating capacity of 1,282. In 1956 it was under the management of E.V. Walls prices of admission then were 1s to 2s 8d. It closed on the 10th November 1979 with the films "Beyond Waikiki" (U) and "Lord of the Rings" (A). It has been a leisure centre now for a number of years.

Paul Henreid

The COLISEUM THEATRE PICTURE HOUSE, corner of Saltley Road and Nechells Place, Birmingham opened in April 1921 the proprietors being MacDonald, Wheatcroft and Tyler, prior to that it was the Coliseum Theatre and before that the Carlton Theatre. It was under the management of Geo. Wm. Bailey. It closed in the early 1940's.

Lana Turner

The CORONET CINEMA, Coventry Road, Small Heath, Birmingham was opened on Saturday 5th August 1922 by the film actress Margo Grahame, the films chosen were "Diana of the Crossways" and "The Card". It had a seating capacity of 1,155, the fine orchestra was under the direction of Max Seenor. The manager was Ernest Elleslie. Prices of admission 6d, 9d, 1s and 1s 6d. In 1930 the manager was Sydney H. Last, in 1940 Eddy G. Clifton. Proprietors The Coronet Cinema (Small Heath)Ltd. It had a Western Electric Mirrophonic Sound System installed. It held regular Sunday concerts from which all proceeds were donated to charity. It closed on the 25th May 1963 showing the films, "Meet the Keystone Cops" (U) with Abbott & Costello and "Tara Son the Cochise" (U).

The CROWN SUPER CINEMA, Icknield Port Road, Ladywood, Birmingham opened on the 26th December 1927 the film chosen "Love Me and the World is Mine", with Norman Kerry and Mary Philbin. Vocalists Albert E. Townsend and Miss Lilian Kerry were booked for the occasion. The orchestra was under the direction of J. Alexander. Prices of admission Balcony 1/- Floor 6d. Commencing on the 29th December the films chosen were "The Blue Danube" and "The Auctioneer". Do you remember the Tarzan serials shown on Saturday afternoons? The actors who played Tarzan originally were Frank Merrill, Buster Crabbe and Herman Brix (who later changed his name to Bruce Bennett). The real Tarzan was Johnny Weissmuller and Jane was played by Maureen O'Sullivan. 'Boy' was played by Johnny Sheffield. Johnny Weissmuller, an olympic swimming champion, made 18 'Tarzan' films commencing with 'Tarzan the Ape Man' and concluding with 'Tarzan and the Mermaids' in 1946. He died aged 79 in Acapulco, Mexico in January 1984. In the 1950's the manager was M.A. Knee. Proprietors ABC Circuit. Closure came on Saturday 14th January 1961 with the showing of the films, "Angry Red Planet" (A) with Gerald Mohr and "Escape of the Amethyst" (U) with Richard Todd.

The COTTERIDGE PICTUREDROME, Hudsons Drive, Cotteridge, Birmingham, opened in 1911, proprietor W.H. Mason. It was later taken over by the Cotteridge Picturedrome Ltd. and under the management of F.W. Pullin. It had a seating capacity of 480. On Sundays it gave 'Grand Sacred Concerts'. It closed circa 1920.

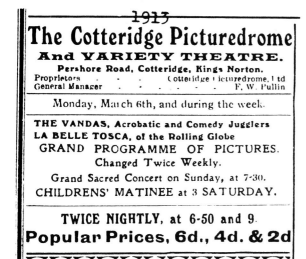

The DANILO CINEMA, Bristol Road South, Birmingham was opened on Saturday 28th January 1939 by Lord Austin. It had a seating capacity of 1,550, the architect was E.S. Roberts. The film chosen was "Test Pilot" (A) with Clarke Gable, Myrna Loy and Spencer Tracey. In 1943 it was managed by A.R. Hudson. It was later re-named the Essoldo. It gave its final performance on Saturday 23rd November 1968, film selected "Barbarella" (X) with Jane Fonda and John Phillip Law. It has been a Bingo and Social Club for a number of years since closure.

This photograph was taken in 1930 by Thomas Cox.

Jean Kent

The DELICIA CINEMA, (The House of Delights), Gosta Green, Birmingham, gave its first public performance on the 5th November 1923 with the film, "The Famous Mrs Fair"., it had an illuminated fountain display at each performance. The orchestra was under the direction of Raymond De Courcy. Seating capacity 1,110. When the film "Sweeney Todd the Barber" was shown, during this early period, the manager William Seeley had real pastry pies made and displayed in the foyer in order to promote the film. One day, a tramp walked in, picked up a pie and proceeded to eat it, he was unaware that the filling was sawdust, however he liked the pastry and proceeded to pocket several of the 'pies' and walked out, much to the amazement of Albert Seeley, the projectionist and brother of the manager, who witnessed the event but did not have the heart to rebuke him, times were very hard then. (To refresh the readers memory, the film was a factual melodrama of a murderer who made and sold pies containing his victims remains). It closed in 1946 but in 1951, Festival of Britain Year, the Birmingham Council purchased the property for £25,000 and converted it into a theatre, this was short lived and the premises were used as a Boxing venue, B.B.C. T.V. Studio and in recent years as an Art Centre. It is now run by the University of Aston, which is in close proximity, as a Studio.

Marilyn Monroe (born Norma Jean Baker) died under mysterious circumstances on the 5th August 1962.

The DUDLEY ROAD CINEMA, situated on the corner of Dudley Road and Chiswell Road, Winson Green, Birmingham opened in 1912 under the management of A. Ferguson, he was later superseded by William Bull. Seating capacity 403. Proprietors Birmingham Picture House Co.Ltd. It closed in 1932 when the Grove Cinema opened which was only 500 yards away. For a number of years now it has been a School of Ballroom Dancing originally opened by Philip Hawley.

Rita Hayworth

The ERA PICTURE PLAYHOUSE, Bordesley Green, Birmingham opened in 1914 under the management of Joseph Drew. It had a seating capacity of 700. Prices of admission 3d & 6d. In 1943 it was under the management of J.H. Hodge and in 1947 William Partridge. When this photograph was taken in 1934 the film being shown was "Hide Out" with Robert Montgomery, Edward Arnold, Maureen O'Sullivan and Mickey Rooney. Closure came on Saturday 21st March 1959 with the showing of the epic film, "Bridge on the River Kwai" (U) with Alec Guinness, Jack Hawkins and William Holden, plus "Pirates of Tripoli" (U) with Paul Henreid and Patricia Medina.

Joan Leslie

The EDGBASTON CINEMA, 233/235 Monument Road, Edgbaston, Birmingham, opened on the 24th December 1928 under the management of J. Windsor Stevenson who was previously at the Adelphi Cinema. The feature film chosen was "The Gaucho" with Douglas Fairbanks and the supporting film "the Gay Defenders" with Richard Dix. It had a seating capacity of 1,616. Roy Page, the well known organist played the fine organ installed. In 1943 it was under the management of F. Jakes. Closure came on Saturday 16th November 1968 with the showing of the film, "Camelot" (U) with Richard Harris and Vanessa Redgrave. It opened as a Music Hall and Bingo Club shortly afterwards but this only lasted a few years and the building was demolished.

Norma Shearer

The ELECTRIC THEATRE, 400 Coventry Road, Small Heath, Birmingham, opened in 1910, proprietors Electric Theatres (1908)Ltd. under the management of G.D. Bradbury. Seating capacity 460. It was re-named CASINO CINEMA and re-opened on Saturday 23rd December 1916 film selected "Isle of Love". Proprietor Harry H. Reynolds, Manager Philip G. Jacobs he was superseded by Albert J. Gale a few months later. Prices of admission 2½d, 4d and 7d. It held daily matinees and two changes of performance weekly. It closed in 1921. The Grange Cinema was erected next door to the Co-operative building in which this cinema was established and this can be seen in the background of the Grange photograph.

THE ELITE CINEMA
BORDESLEY GREEN

The
ELITE

Manager
A. R. Smith

PROGRAMME
◇ for ◇
APRIL
1936

Phone
169 VICTORIA

"Elite" Theatre and Billiard Hall, Bordesley Green.

The ELITE CINEMA, situated on the corner of Crown Rd and Bordesley Green, Birmingham, opened on the 9th August 1913 and was then known as the Elite Picture Palace showing General Variety and Pictures. Seating capacity 1,327. Prices of admission 3d & 4d Stalls, 6d in the Lounge. Music was provided by the Melford Trio and Dora Denmark. In 1914 it was managed by James Stockton. The film shown on the 5th August 1914 the day after the first world war was declared, was "Old St. Paul's or the Great Fire of London". It was bombed in the 1940's during the second world war, the last film shown was, "Passport to Fame" starring Edward G. Robinson and Jean Arthur.

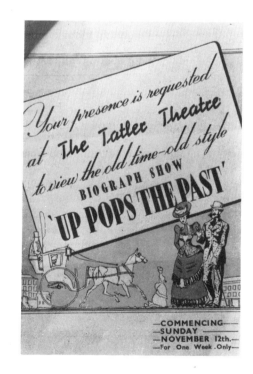

Jean Simmons

The ELITE CINEMA, Soho Road, Handsworth, Birmingham opened on Monday 30th September 1913, proprietor Mrs Lizzie Mann, the film chosen being, "Bread Cast upon the Water". Prices of admission Grand Balcony 1/- Floor 3d & 6d. Seating capacity 870. It closed in the early 1970's after being an Asian cinema for a number of years.

Wallace Beery

The interior of a mystery cinema in Birmingham, top, as it was originally and opposite, after being refurbished. Note the luxurious decor. Can you name it?

ERDINGTON

Hedy Lamarr

The ERDINGTON EMPIRE PALACE, corner of Orphanage and Edwards Road, Erdington, Birmingham opened in 1911 under the management of Robert C. Richards, he was superseded by Lionel J. Harrison and Augustus Collins when it closed in 1918. The photograph was taken when it was a Skating Rink prior to opening as a cinema. Proprietors Erdington Skating Rink Co.Ltd. In 1914 it was known as the New Erdington Picture Playhouse.

The GRAND PICTURE HOUSE, 236 Alum Rock Road, (corner of Langton Road) Birmingham opened on the 14th March 1914 advertising as showing of All Star Pictures. Prices of admission 3d, 6d in the stalls and 9d in the balcony. It was managed by Helsby Wright and had a seating capacity of 950. It closed on Saturday 29th August 1959, films selected "Snowfire" (U) and "Sabu and the Magic Ring" (U) manager F.P. Cozens. Proprietors Saltley Grand Picture House Co. It later opened as a motor service station.

Bette Davis

Michael
O'Shaughnessy

Betty Hutton

The GAIETY PICTURE HOUSE, Coleshill Street, Birmingham, was previously a music hall and theatre, it opened as a cinema in the 1920's. In the late 1930's it was almost burnt down and after restoration and alteration it re-opened on Monday the 18th December 1939 showing the films "Lucky Night" (A) with Robert Taylor and Myrna Loy and "Black Eyes" (A) with Mary Maguire and Otto Kruger. Prices of admission 6d and 1/3. It had a seating capacity of 1,487. It closed on the 29th November 1969 with the film, "The Killing of Sister George" (X) with Beryl Reid, Susanna York and Coral Browne.

The GRANGE SUPER CINEMA, corner of Grange and Coventry Road, Small Heath, Birmingham. The original building was erected in 1915 but re-built in 1922. It had a seating capacity of 1,310. Proprietors Coronet Cinema (Small Heath)Ltd. In 1940 it was managed by A.P.R. Crombleholme, he was followed by E.T. Bennett. Prices of admission in 1957 ranged from 1/- to 2/4. It closed on the 31st October 1959 showing the film "April Love" starring Pat Boone and Shirley Jones, the manager was then R. Butcher.

Miss Simms, manageress and chief sales lady at the Grange, taken a few days before the cinema closed.

1913

Globe Electric Theatre

BARTON'S ARMS, ASTON.

TELEPHONE NORTHERN 652.

Twice Nightly, 7 and 9.

Up-to-Date Pictures   Delightful Music.

Week commencing Monday, November 3rd

Mon., Tues. and Wed.——

HEROES OF THE MINE

also "Arson at Sea."

Thur., Fri. and Sat.——

ALONE IN THE JUNGLE

The GLOBE PICTURE PALACE, 139 High Street, (corner of New Street and opposite the Barton Arms, Public House) Aston, Birmingham, opened on Monday 4th August 1913, it was then known as The Globe Electric Theatre. Seating capacity 700, manager Gilbert V. Butler he was superseded by Charles E. Pinder and Francis W. Robbins in 1920. The film chosen was "The Heritage". Prices of admission 3d to 9d. It closed in September 1955.

THE GRAND PICTURE PALACE
Soho Road, Handsworth.

Proprietors	- The C.G.H.S. Cinema Co. Ltd.
Manager	Mr. Frederick Jeffrey

GREAT SUCCESS

OF THE NEW GRAND PICTURE PALACE,
OPEN DAILY 5 to 10-30 p.m.
Continuous Performance.

Programme changed TWICE WEEKLY,
Monday and Thursday.

The most comfortable and up to date Theatre in the Midlands. All the latest subjects will be shown on the screen from time to time, making the programme one of the most complete entertainments extant.

"THE TALISMAN"

A Great Picture founded upon Sir Walter Scott's Novel.

LA TOSCA, A French Tragedy.

POPULAR PRICES— 3d. & 6d. GRAND LOUNGE, 1/-

THE ENTERTAINMENT FOR THE FAMILY.

Shirley Maclaine

The GRAND PICTURE PALACE, 263 Soho Road, Handsworth, Birmingham was opened on Wednesday 27th September 1911 by T.H. Berry Esquire, (Chairman of the District Council) admission was by ticket only. Entertainment was provided by Madam Laura Taylor. Proprietors C.G.H.C. Cinema Co.Ltd., manager appointed Frederick Jeffrey. Seating capacity 800. Prices of admission, ground floor 3d & 6d, Grand Lounge 1/-. In 1936 it was under the management of Albert Colman. It closed in 1982 after being an Asian Cinema for a number of years.

Van Johnson

The GREAT HAMPTON PICTURE PALACE, situated on the corner of Livery and Kenyon Street, Birmingham, was opened on the afternoon of the 28th November 1912, by Alderman A.C. Hayes, Mr. Brooks, the managing director of the company was presiding. It had a seating capacity of 700. The manager appointed was Joe Melman. The public were admitted to the Evening performance as the opening ceremony was by invitation only. The proprietors in the period 1924 to 1930 were Excellent Cinema (1924) Ltd., the manager was then John Dunn Steal. In 1930 it was taken overy by Hampton Cinemas Ltd., and the manager appointed F.E. Williams. It closed in the early 1930's and has been industrial premises ever since.

THE NEW GREEN LANE CINEMA

presents

It's Monthly Programme

OCTOBER 1939

Manager MR. CLIVE JENKINS

Telephone: 612

The GREEN LANE PICTURE HOUSE, Green Lane, Small Heath, Birmingham opened on the 2nd February 1914 rendering a first class programme of pictures and music, under the management of Albert Clayton. Just prior to the opening date the roof fell in, this naturally caused some delay but, fortunately no-one was hurt. Prices of admission 4d to 8d. Seating capacity 900. In 1935 it was modernised and re-opened as "The New Green Lane Cinema" under the management of E.H. Neighbour, he was superseded by Clive Jenkins, W.H. Evans and J.H. Alexander. Proprietors G.L. Cinema Ltd. It closed circa 1957.

The GROVE CINEMA, 473 Dudley Road, Winson Green, Birmingham opened on the 22nd August 1932. The film chosen for the opening ceremony was "Arsene Lupin" starring John and Lionel Barrymore. In 1943 it was under the management of G. Martin, prices of admission then ranged from 1/- to 2/3d. In 1962 it was managed by E.E. Kent. It closed on Saturday 24th October 1981, films chosen, "Happy Birthday to Me" (X) with Melissa Sue Anderson and Glenn Ford and "Used Cars" (AA).

Ingrid Bergman

The HARBORNE PICTURE PALACE, Serpentine Road, Harborne, Birmingham. Opened in 1913 the proprietors being, Bosco's Pictures Ltd., the manager was Bert Dawes. In 1920 it was W. Jeffs. Prices of admission then being 6d to 1/-. It had a seating capacity of 903. In the 1940's it was taken over by Denman (Midland) Cinemas Ltd and in the 1950's by C.M.A. Ltd. When it closed on the 13th April 1957, showing the films, "Town on Trial" (A) with John Mills and Charles Coburn plus the film "Repirsal" it was an A.B.C. house.

The HEATH PICTURE PALACE, situated on the corner of Washwood Heath and Bennetts Road, Saltley, Birmingham, it was opened on the 17th January 1914 under the management of W.G. Horton.   Builders E. Garfields Ltd., Architect A. Hurley Robinson A.R.I.B.A.   Prices of admission 2d, 4d and 6d.   It had a small orchestra, violin, piano and Cello.   Seating capacity 724.   The films chosen were, "In The Middle of the Jungle", "Keeping Husbands at Home", "Pearl as a Clairvoyant" and "The Girl in the Cabinet".   Note the lettering on the photograph, 'Line up 2d & 4d' on the one side and 'Line up 6d' on the other.   In 1936 it was under the management of J. Rutter but when it closed in 1940 it was under the management of C. Watson.   It later opened as an antique shop and later as a Fancy Goods Warehouse.

Robert Walker

The HIGHGATE PICTURE PALACE, situated on the corner of Darwin and Hollier Street, Birmingham, opened on Friday 17th October 1913 under the management of Thomas Frederick Clamp.   It had a seating capacity of 850.   In 1921 it was managed by E.C. Kirms.   In 1924 it ran a serial entitled, "Green Archer" which was looked forward to weekly by the locals.   Admission was 1p in the lower portion and 4p in the raised portion.   It was demolished in 1959 under a re-development scheme.

The IDEAL PICTURE HOUSE, 106 High Street, Kings Heath, Birmingham opened in 1915 under the management of Ernest Ellerslie. It had a seating capacity of 542. Prices of admission ranged from 5d to 9d. It was licensed for Music. In 1921 it published, for the benefit of patrons, the "Ideal" monthly bulletin price 2d. Although the actual building was in York Road the entrance was down a long passage in High Street, at the side of the Hare & Hounds Public House. Other managers were Mrs Lilian Lord and Augustus Collins. It was equipped for sound and, prior to its closure in April 1932 showed the following talkies, "Moby Dick" with John Barrymore and Joan Bennett, "Born to Love" with Constance Bennett, "A Matrimonial Problem" with Frank Kay and "Trader Horn" with Edwina Booth and Harry Carey.

The IMPERIAL PICTURE PALACE, 516 Moseley Road, Birmingham opened on Monday 26th January 1914 showing the films, "Satan's Castle" and John Bunny in "The Pirates". Proprietor Henry Grigg. It had a fine orchestra under the direction of Paul Rimmer. In the publication "FILMS", the cinema trade journal, dated 13th April 1916 the following was inserted: "You are always sure of a high class and pleasing programme at the little Imperial in Moseley Road, over whose destinies George L. Harris presided with so much eclate". In 1921 it was managed by W.E. Maund. Prices of admission then varied from 6d to 1/-., proprietor then was Mrs. J. Grigg. It closed in 1983.

W—I—J

List of Streets and Places in Birmingham and District.	Which Car to take.	Central Depart and Arrive Termini.	Where to get off or on Car, and Right or Left turns to take for Street or Place required.	Ordin. Fare.
				d.
FOR				
Homer st, Balsall Hth..	Moseley ..	High st or Hill st	Cars pass	1
§Homœopathic Hospital, 15, Easy row				
Hooper st, Dudley rd..	Dudley rd..	Edmund st ..	Cars pass	1
Hope st, Gooch st ..	Cannon Hill	Lr Temple st ..	Cars pass	1
Horse Fair ..	Selly Oak ..	Navigation st ..	Tram route ..	1
§Horse Mkt., Smithfield				
Hospital st, Summer ln	Handsw'rth	Colmore row ..	Summer lane, 2L	1
Howard rd,Coventry rd	Yardley ..	Station st ..	Cars pass ..	2
Howard rd, Hdswrth..	Perry Barr	Martineau st ..	Wellington rd, 3R..	2
Howard rd ..	Alcester lane	High st or Hill st	Cars pass ..	2
Howard st, Hampton st	Handsw'rth	Colmore row ..	Cars pass ..	1
Howard st, Smethwick	Soho ..	Edmund st ..	3R from terminus ..	1½
Howe st, Curzon st ..	Saltley ..	Martineau st ..	Cars pass ..	1
Hubert rd, Selly Oak..	Selly Oak..	Navigation st ..	Cars pass ..	1½
Hubert st, Aston rd..	Aston Cross	Steelhouse lane	Cars pass ..	1
Hugh rd, Small Heath	Coventry rd	Sta. st or High st	Charles rd, 4L	1
Hume st, Smethwick..	Dudley rd..	Edmund st ..	Windmill lane	1½
Humpage rd, Bdsl'y Gn	Bordsl'y Gn	High st ..	Cars pass ..	1
Hunters rd, Hckly hill	Handsw'rth	Colmore row ..	Farm st, 1L..	1
Hunters vale, Hockley	Handsw'rth	Colmore row ..	Farm st, 2L..	1
Hunton hl, Gravelly h.	Erdington	Steelhouse lane	Cars pass ..	1½
Hunton rd, Gravelly hl	Erdington	Steelhouse lane	Hunton hill, 2 R	1½
Hunts rd, Stirchley ..	K's Norton	Navigation st ..	Cars pass ..	2
Hurst st, Smallbrook	Balsall H'th	Lr Temple st ..	Tram route ..	1
Hutton st, Handswrth	Perry Barr	Martineau st ..	Livingstone rd, 3R, 1L	
Hutton st, Saltley ..	Washw'd H	Martineau st ..	Cars pass ..	1
Hyde rd, Ladywood ..	Ladyw'd rd	Lr Temple st ..	Cars pass ..	1
Hylton st, Vyse st ..	Handsw'rth	Colmore row ..	Vyse st, 1R ..	1
Icknield Port rd, Ldyw	Ladyw'd rd	Lr Temple st ..	Tram route ..	1
Icknield sq, Ladywood	Ladyw'd rd	Lr Temple st ..	Monument rd, 2L ..	1
Icknield st, Hockley {	Lodge rd ..	Edmund st ..	Cars pass ..	1
	Handsw'rth	Colmore row ..	Cars pass ..	1
Imperial rd, Bordesley	Bordsl'y Gn	High st ..	Cars pass ..	1
Inge st, Essex st ..	Balsall H'th	Lr Temple st ..	Cars pass ..	1
Ingleby st, Ladywood	Dudley rd..	Edmund st ..	Cars pass ..	1
Inglewood rd,Sparkhill	Stratford rd	Sta. st or High st	Cars pass ..	1
Inkerman st, Aston Newtown	Perry Barr	Martineau st ..	Cars pass	1
Inkerman st, Vauxhall	Washw'd H	Martineau st ..	Duddeston mill rd, 2R	1
§Inland Revenue Office, Paradise st				
Institute rd, Kings Hth	K's Heath..	High st or Hill st	Cars pass ..	2
*Iron lane, Stechford ..				
Irving rd ..	Erdington	Steelhouse lane	Wheelwright rd	1½
Irving st, Horse Fair..	Selly Oak ..	Navigation st ..	Cars pass ..	1
Island rd, Handsworth	Handsw'rth	Colmore row ..	Cars pass ..	2
Islington row, Five W's	Ladyw'd rd	Lr Temple st ..	Tram route ..	1
Ivor rd, Sparkhill ..	Stoney lane	Station st ..	Cars pass ..	1
*Ivy House ln, Hall Grn				
Ivy lane, Lawley st ..	Bordsl'y Gn	High st ..	Cars pass ..	1
Ivy rd, Stirchley ..				
Ivy rd, Handsworth ..	Handsw'rth	Colmore row ..	Whitehall rd, 1R	1
Jackson rd ..	Alum Rock	Martineau st ..	3R from terminus..	1
Jaffray Hospital ..	Erdington	Steelhouse lane	Jaffray rd cont'd ..	2
Jaffray rd, Erdington	Erdington	Steelhouse lane	Cars pass ..	2
Jakeman rd, Balsall Heath	Balsall H'th	Lr Temple st ..	Cars pass ..	1

* No Tram service near this Street or Place at present.
§ This Street or Place is situate in the immediate centre of Birmingham.

The KINGS HEATH PICTURE HOUSE, Ruskin Hall, 25 Institute Road, Kings Heath, Birmingham opened in 1911 the proprietors being Kings Heath Electric Pictures Ltd., the manager & secretary being A.H. Allen. In 1915 it changed its name to COSY CINEMA and was then under the management of Lawson Trout. It was only operative for a few years. The above advertisement was inserted in the Offical Tramways & Street Guide of Birmingham of that period and is included for the readers interest.

This is the type of ticket that was issued to passengers during this period. Note the advertisement on the reverse side of the ticket.

THE KINGS NORTON
CINEMA
Proprietors - - - The Kings Norton Picture House Co. Ltd.
Licensee and Manager - - - Mr. C. Maurice Richards.

SOUVENIR PROGRAMME
of the
OPENING

SATURDAY,
APRIL 16th
1938

THE KINGS NORTON CINEMA

Opening Programme
Saturday, April 16th, 1938

1. National Anthem

2. Coloured Cartoon

3.
JEANETTE   NELSON
MacDONALD   EDDY
in
MAYTIME ®
with
JOHN BARRYMORE

A Musical Romance that will Live Long in the Memory.

Errol Flynn

The KINGS NORTON CINEMA, opened on the 16th April 1938, the film selected was "MAYTIME" (see copy programme) The manager was C. Maurice Richards. It had a seating capacity of, in the auditorium 850, balcony 280. It was fitted with the latest Western Electric Microphonic Sound System. It closed on the 15th June 1983 showing the film "TOOTSIE" (PG) starring Dustin Hoffman.

Loretta Young
(born Gretchen Belzer)

Gregory Peck

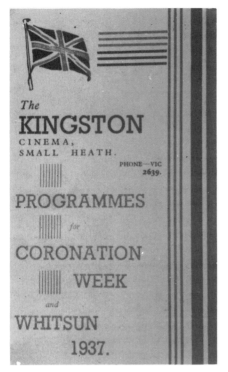

The KINGSTON CINEMA, Coventry Road, Small Heath, Birmingham opened on the 4th August 1935, the ceremony was performed by E.J. Bryant, Esq. The film chosen was "Ruggles of Red Gap", starring Charles Laughton and Mary Boland. Seating capacity 1,475, it had a spacious balcony and roomy lounge. The builders were W.J. Whittal & Sons., Architect Ronald Satchwell. Proprietors Coronet Cinema (Small Heath)Ltd., In 1940 it was under the management of A. Dowding. The final performance was given on Saturday 14th December 1968 with the showing of the films, "Prudence and the Pill" (X) with David Niven and Deborah Kerr and "Witchcraft" (X) with Jack Hedley and Lon Chaney Jnr. It had a Western Electric Sound System Wide Range installed. For a number of years now it has been a Social Club run by the Ladbrooke organisation.

The KINGSWAY CINEMA, High Street, Kings Heath, Birmingham opened on the 2nd March 1925 under the management of J.H. Richardson. The film chosen for the grand opening was "Down to the Sea in Ships", see copy programme for full details. Prices of admission Balcony 1/6 and 1/- Ground floor and Stalls 8d and 6d. It had a seating capacity of 1,362. It closed on the 3rd May 1980 showing the films "The Bermuda Triangle" (U) and "Encounter with Disaster" (A) and under the management of L.A. Gibbons.

The LOZELLS PICTURE HOUSE, 56 Lozells Road, Birmingham opened in 1911 under the management of Augustus Collins. Prices of admission 5d & 9d. It was re-built in 1922 and officially opened on Saturday 23rd December of that year, those present being the Lord Mayor, Alderman David Davis, Alderman F. Smith, J.P. and The Rev. T. Kilby Champness. All proceeds from the special programme were donated to the Lord Mayor's Distress Fund. On Monday 26th December (Boxing Day) it advertised a Grand Opening showing the film, "Saturday Night", supported by "Married Life". Seating capacity now being 1,000. It had a fine orchestra under the direction of Paul Rimmer. A few years later a Wurlitzer Organ was installed, the first organist being Ernest Newman. It is generally accepted that he was the first to broadcast on a provincial cinema organ in 1927, broadcasting by the Paul Rimmer, from this cinema was also a popular event. Another popular oganist was Edwin Godbold. On the 28th July 1942, while showing the film, "Honky Tonk" starring Clarke Gable, Lana Turner and Frank Morgan, it was completely destroyed by enemy action during an air raid in the second world war, the manager, Lionel Jennings, who was on fire watch duty, was killed.

LADYWOOD PICTURE PALACE, 21 Morville Street, Birmingham opened in June 1910 (see advertisement for details) it was one of the first suburban cinemas to be opened, it closed circa 1914 when the Ledsam Picture House opened in Ledsam Street, which was only 250 yards away.

The LYRIC PICTURE PLAYHOUSE, Edward Street, Parade, Birmingham opened in 1910, it was then known as The Queens Picture House, previously it had been a Theatre of renown, known as The Queens Theatre. After refurbishment it opened as The Lyric on the 22nd September 1919, the opening ceremony was performed by Alderman Jephcott M.P., the film chosen was, "Wheel of Life" with Pauline Frederick. Prices of admission 1/- in the balcony, 9d & 6d downstairs. Seating capacity 950. One of the early managers was Walter Payne, from 1920 to 1927, H. Harrison and in 1935 Grahame Hylton. It gave its final performance on Saturday 10th October 1960, films chosen, "Ivanhoe" (U) with Robert and Elizabeth Taylor and "Mail Van Murder" (U). Prior to opening as a theatre it was the Church of Christ the Saviour, built by George Dawson, M.A. in 1847.

The MAYPOLE CINEMA, Alcester Road South, Birmingham opened on Sunday 1st August 1937 with the film, "Keep your seats Please", with George Formby. It had a seating capacity of 738 in the auditorium and 377 in the balcony. The architect was E.S. Roberts. In 1943 it was under the management of Harry Stanford. Prices of admission 6d, 9d and 1/-. It closed on the 26th January 1961 with the showing of the film, "The Lost World" with Claude Rains and Michael Rennie, an apt title for the building was then demolished to make way for a modern shopping complex.

"What would Saturday morning have been without our trip to the Maypole for the Saturday matinee? I was lucky in that I had an older brother who used to get there before me and save me a seat.

What happy times we spent with Roy Rogers, Gene Autrey, Hopalong Cassidy, Flash Gordon and my favourite, Zorro. Many's the happy hours I've spent hanging over cliffs and being locked in dungeons with the roof and walls closing in on me. How would I last out until next Saturday to find out how my hero would escape — which he always did?

I can also remember, with pride, the day I was made an ABC Minor — complete with badge. I think we also had some sort of certificate with our names on, but this has long since vanished.

Apart from the Saturday matinee, complete with brother, my mother and I went to the Maypole twice each week. In those days, of course, the programme changed frequently, but the best part about it all was the fact that on the way home we always called into the Maypole pub where my father would send us out into the corridor a half pint of shandy for my mother and a glass of Vimto for me. I thought this very daring!

However, the memory of the dear old Maypole which sticks in my mind is of the lushness of the decor and the lovely smell of air freshener, or whatever it was they used. Just to walk through the door was to go into another world of plush and perfume.

Of course, it is now just another block of shops but to me it will always be the Saturday chorus of "Watch out, he's behind you!.!."

Sheila Rawlins
Sparkhill, Birmingham

Eddie Bracken

Sally Gray

The MAYFAIR CINEMA, College Road, Kingstanding, Birmingham opened on Monday 14th September 1931, film chosen, "The Middle Watch" with Owen Nares and Dodo Watts. Architect W.H. Weeden, proprietors Mayfair Cinema (Birmingham)Ltd. In 1957 prices of admission ranged from 1/- to 2/3d. Closure came on Saturday 25th January 1964 with the showing of the films, "Blood of the Warrior" (A) and "Road Racers" (U). The building was later demolished.

This film was made in 1941

The MODEL PICTURE HOUSE, 271-273 Coventry Road, Small Heath, Birmingham, when it opened in 1911 it was under the management of S. Wright and was called The Small Heath Picture House, it changed to Model in 1914. It was a very popular venue for the locals especially the children when special matinees were held, admission one penny. The performance was always preceded by a good sing song with the pianist. In 1923 five regular patrons, Mr Judd, Bayliss, Hartle, Hall and Peters, who were rather large in proportion, booked regular seats with the manager, W.H. Fisher for the Monday and Saturday performances, however, owing to their size they could not fit in the normal seating so he arranged to have double seating in the back row of the balcony to accommodate them. In 1928 the proprietors were Reynolds, Garfield and Reynolds. The cinema closed in 1931 and the premises were taken over by Loo Bloom the Tailors.

Harold Lloyd

The MOSELEY PICTURE HOUSE, 345-347 Moseley Road, Birmingham opened on Monday 12th May 1913, film selected "Oedipus Rex". Proprietor A.E. Parry. Prices of admission 3d, 6d & 9d. Seating capacity 650. In 1943 it was managed by Joseph Levey. In August 1958, after the lease had expired, the premises were badly damaged by fire, it was almost rebuilt and refurbished by V.L. Parry, the son of the original owner. In its latter years it was an Asian cinema, finally the premises were demolished, owing to a road widening scheme, in 1974.

Danny Kaye

Nechells Picture Palace,

Proprietor:
H. GOODMAN.

Manager:
F. J. ROBBINS.

BLOOMSBURY STREET,

BIRMINGHAM.

Sep 1915

Messrs. Moss Empires Ltd

Dear Sir

I should like to congratulate you on the Presentation of your film "The Dare Devil Circus Queen" at the above house am pleased to say that the film proved the greatest house filler ever shown here under my managment;

Faithfully Yours
Frank Robbins
General Manager

This letter was published in the publication 'FILMS'
the Cinema Trade Journal on September 23, 1915.

The NECHELLS PICTURE PALACE, Bloomsbury Street, Nechells, Birmingham was opened on the 24th June 1911 at 3.00 p.m., with a Splendid Programme of Up-To-Date Pictures, prices of admission 6d, 4d & 2d. Prior to opening as a cinema it was the Oddfellows Hall which was completely re-designed by the architect Harry H. Reynolds and opened as a full time cinema, he was also the Managing Director of the cinema. This was the week when citizens all over the Country were celebrating the Coronation of King George V. It was later taken over by H. Goodman and managed by F.J. Robbins. It closed circa 1916.

Gary Cooper

The NEWTOWN PALACE, New Town Row, Aston, Birmingham opened on Monday 5th January 1914, advertising High Class Pictures and Select Variety. It could accommodate 2,000. Prices of admission 2d, 3d, 4d & 6d. Proprietors Moss Empires Ltd. It had a full size stage and seven dressing rooms. It closed on Saturday 22nd April 1961 showing the films "Giant Claw" (X) with Boris Karloff and Tom Duggan. Since closure it has had a varied existance, it was finally a Bingo and Social Club run by Ladbrookes Ltd., this closed in 1983.

Lucille Ball

Cary Grant
(born Archie Leach)

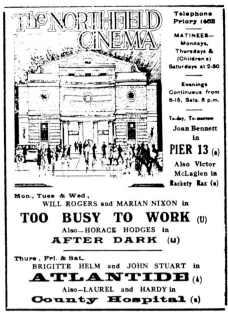

The NORTHFIELD CINEMA, Bristol Road South, Birmingham, opened on the 4th February 1929, the film chosen was, "The Triumph of the Scarlet Pimpernel", starring Matherson Lang. It was under the management of Harold Cecil Pickering. Seating capacity 1,200. It had a first class orchestra under the direction of Arthur Montgomery. Prices of admission ranged from 6d to 1/6d. The architect was Major Lewis R. McFarlane and built by B. Whitehouse & Sons Ltd. When it closed on Saturday 2nd June 1962 the manager, R. Voyce, chose the films "Blood of the Vampire" (X) with Donald Wolfit and "Grip of the Strangler" (X) with Boris Karloff.

HIGH SOCIETY, starring Frank Sinatra, Bing Crosby, Grace Kelly, Celeste Holm and Louis Armstrong, was the biggest moneymaker film of 1956, songs to be remembered are 'True Love', 'I Love You Samantha', 'Who wants to be a Millionaire' and 'Well, Did you Evah'.

A DETAIL OF THE FRIEZE IN THE FOYER.

The OAK CINEMA, 763 Bristol Road, (corner of Chapel Lane) Selly Oak, Birmingham opened on Monday 4th February 1924 with the showing of the film, "Chu Chin Chow". It was built for the Selly Oak Pictures Ltd., architect Harold S. Scott, manager T. Gathercole who was superseded by H. Bliss Hill. It had a seating capacity of 900 in the auditorium and 300 in the balcony. In 1935 it closed for enlargement and refurbishment and re-opened on the 16th December 1935 under the management of W.A.G. Grieve. The films chosen were "George White's Scandals" (U) with Alice Faye and James Dunn, and "The Flame Within" (A) with Ann Harding and Herbert Marshall. Prices of admission being 6d, 1/-, 1/3 and 1/6. In 1936 the film, "Under Two Flags" was shown, (see photograph) with Ronald Colman and Claudette Colbert. The frieze was modelled from the old Pompeian examples and represented a triumphal procession of the arts and crafts. In July 1951, when managed by Roy A. Fielder, it was voted the second cleanest cinema in the Country and he was presented with a silver medal after the performance, by the chairman of the Birmingham Public Entertainments Committee, A.H. Sayer. Closure came on the 3rd November 1979 with the showing of the films, "Spaceman and King Arthur" (U) with Dennis Dugan, Jim Dale, Ron Moody, Kenneth More and John Le Mesurier and "Dumbo" (U) a Walt Disney Film. The building was demolished in December 1984.

Vincent Price   Dennis Price   Clara Bow

Original building

Marlene Dietrich

New building

The ODEON CINEMA Birchfield Road, Perry Barr, Birmingham opened on the 4th August 1930 films selected "Illusion" with Nancy Carroll and "Dark Red Roses" with Stewart Rome. Prices of admission 6d, 9d, 1/- & 1/3, booking fee 3d extra. It was then known as The Odeon Theatre. This was the first Odeon to be built in Birmingham for Oscar Deutsch by B. Whitehouse & Sons Ltd of Monument Road, Edgbaston. It had a seating capacity of 1,820. The furnishing and fittings were the last word in comfort, indeed as it was in all 'Odeons'. The word Odeon — derived from the greek word ODEUM — symbolises — Oscar Deutsch Entertains Our Nation. It had a fine seventeen piece orchestra, Stanley Pendrous was the senior violinist and played on his pressenda violin. During the war a time bomb lodged beneath the cinema but fortunately this was defused by a bomb disposal unit, Mr Deutsch, in gratitude, had a gold medallion specially struck and presented one to each of the squad which entitled them to a free seat, for life, in any Odeon cinema. Closure came on Saturday 3rd May 1969 with the showing of the films, "The Wrecking Crew" (A) with Dean Martin and "The Big Gundown" (A) with Lee Van Cleef. It later opened as a Top Rank Club. (Mr Deutsch was the chairman of the Cinematograph Exhibitors Association in the 1930's. He died in 1941 at the early age of 48, a victim of cancer)

The ODEON CINEMA, Kettlehouse Road, Kingstanding, Birmingham opened on the 22nd July 1935 by Commander Locker-Lampson, M.P. The architect was Harry W. Weedon. It had a seating capacity of 1,346. The film chosen was, "The Lives of a Bengal Lancer"(U) with Gary Cooper, Franchot Tone and Richard Cromwell. It closed on the 1st December 1962 with the films "To Hell and Back" (A) with Audie Murphy and Marshall Thompson and "The Man Without a Star" (A) with Kirk Douglas and Jeanne Crain. Proceeds from this event were donated to the Royal Cripples Hospital. (below depicts the interior) It later opened as a Leisure Centre and Bingo establishment.

Richard Carlson, Hedy Lamarr and
Walter Pidgeon from the 1942 film
"WHITE CARGO".

Brian Donlevy

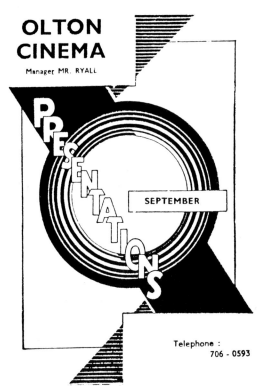

OLTON CINEMA

Manager MR. RYALL

PRESENTATIONS

SEPTEMBER

Telephone :
706 - 0593

The OLTON CINEMA, Warwick Road, Olton, Birmingham opened on the 2nd October 1933 under the management of Walter F. Neal the film chosen was "Falling For You" with Jack Hulbert & Douglas Furber. It had a seating capacity of 1,420. When it closed on the 16th September 1972 it was under the management of Billy Ryall, the chief projectionist was Jack Line. The film chosen was "The Lady in the Car with Glasses and a Gun" (AA) with Samantha Eggar & Oliver Reed. Shortly afterwards the property was demolished and an office block erected on the site.

This film was made in 1933

The ORIENT CINEMA, 32/40 High Street, Aston, Birmingham opened on the 4th August 1930 by John Maxwell Esq., it was designed and ornamented in Eastern Style, it had a beautifully decorated proscenium and drop curtain. The film chosen being "The Cohens and The Kellys in Scotland", with Charles Murray and George Sidney. It had a seating capacity of 1,544. The manager in 1937 was Alex. Simpson. It gave its final performance on Sunday 2nd February 1964 with the showing of the film "Thing That Couldn't Die" (X).

Herbert Marshall

The PALACE CINEMA, 96 High Street, Erdington, Birmingham opened on the 24th December 1912, the General Manager was W.E. Steven, F.R.C.A., prices of admission, Grand Circle 9d, Stalls 6d. It had an 'Efficient Orchestra'. In 1920 it was managed by Victor C. Hornblow and in 1921 by Alec Stannard. From 1928 to 1933 it was managed by Frank Riego, (who went to manage the Plaza Cinema, Stockland Green). It had a seating capacity of 1,320. Prior to opening as a cinema it was the Erdington Public Hall. Closure came on the 19th August 1972, when it was managed by John Goody, the films chosen were, "Oliver" (U) with Ron Moody, Oliver Reed and Harry Secombe.

The PICTURE HOUSE, 67 High Street, Erdington, Birmingham opened on the afternoon of Saturday 18th October 1913 to an invited audience, the ceremony was performed by Mr E. Cheshire, J.P. (President of the Childrens Hospital) Tea was provided and a silver collection taken in aid of the Hospital. The manager was Bertram Murray, Architect A.H. Hamblin. Seating capacity between 500 and 600. The public were invited to the Evening Performance but on Monday 20th a special film was shown entitled "African Hunt", it was a celebrated motion picture of that period. The cinema was built at the rear of the Swan Hotel with the entrance in the High Street. The proprietors were West's Picture Playhouse Ltd. This establishment and the Palace were later acquired by Chas H. Dent but were later taken over by the ABC Circuit.
Closure came on the 24th November 1956 with the showing of the films "Charlie Moon (U) with Max Bygrave and "The Village" (U). It was then under the management of Mrs. A. Ashmore.

HUMPHREY BOGART — born 15/12/1899, the star who became a legend in his life time, married Lauren Bacall (born 16/9/1924) on the 22/5/1945 at a private ceremony in Missouri, U.S.A., after starring with her in the film, "To Have and Have Not", in 1944, this being his fourth marriage. Lauren was only 20 and until 18 months before had been an unknown cinema usherette. He died at 2.10 a.m. on the 14/1/1957.

Humphrey Bogart

Lauren Bacall

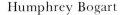

The PALACE CINEMA, Summer Hill Road, Spring Hill, Birmingham opened on the 18th December 1911, it was then called The Palace Theatre and was advertised as showing beautiful Motion Pictures, Illustrated song and Selected Variety, the films chosen were, "Christmas Carol" and "Tired and Absent Minded Man". Twice nightly performances 6.45 and 9.00. Prices of admission 2d, 3d, 4d and 6d. Proprietors Moss Empires Ltd. In the 1930's it was taken over by the ABC circuit. It had a seating capacity of 861. It closed in 1941 and was taken over by Bulpit & Sons Ltd. The building was demolished in 1981 and a new factory, Rabone Chesterman Ltd. built on the site in 1984.

Stewart Granger

The PARK LANE PICTURE PALACE, 278 Park Lane, Aston, Birmingham opened in 1911, the proprietor Percy A. Sumner, in 1913 the cinema was taken over by Frederick Kitchin. It was only operative for a few years.

Pavilion Electric Theatre,
WITTON ROAD, ASTON.

Manager .... WALTER M. MILLAR.
Seats can be Booked by Telephone—Nat. 333 East.

The Cosiest and most Picturesque Theatre in the Midlands.

MONDAY, AUGUST 28, 1911.

Twice Nightly, 6 50 & 9. Twice Nightly, 6 50 & 9.
Entire Change of Pictures Mondays and Thursdays.

Perfect Pictures. Popular Prices. Positively the Finest
Performance in Birmingham.

ADDED ATTRACTIONS

SCOTT HASTINGS
The Singing Jester.

Miss FANNY WATSON
Mezzo Soprano in her latest Illustrated Songs.

By Special Request throughout the week.
The Pictures of the 8th Batt'n. Royal Warwick Regiment
in Camp at Towyn.

Our Programme also includes the most
UP-TO-DATE PICTURES Ever Thrown upon a Screen.
Pathos. Comedy, Travel and Drama!

The New Home of Refined Pictures and Varieties.
The Management have secured the very Finest of Animated
Pictures, interspersed with the highest Class of Vaudeville
MATINEE EVERY SATURDAY AT 2·30.
Popular Prices 3d, 6d and 9d.

WHY GO TO THE CITY ?   WE HAVE THE BEST SHOW !

The PAVILION ELECTRIC THEATRE, Witton Road, Aston, Birmingham had a Grand Opening on Easter Monday 17th April 1911 advertising The Finest Animated Pictures and Vaudeville Artists. Manager appointed W.M. Miller. Prices of admission 3d, 6d & 9d. Twice Nightly 7 & 9.00 p.m. The Orchestra was under the direction of Louis Gledhill. It closed in 1915. The building, which is still standing today, has had a varied existence, Social Club, Bingo Hall and Snooker Club.

The PALLADIUM CINEMA, Soho Hill, Hockley, Birmingham. It was originally opened on Wednesday 15th November 1911 and known as the Hockley Picture House and under the management of Bert Wynne. It had a seating capacity of 506. In June 1918 it was under the management of A. Whitworth-Cheetam, an enterprising manager who put on a change of 'STAR' pictures every day for one week plus a strong and up-to-date programme of variety. It was re-built and enlarged in 1922 and called the New Palladium Cinema, it advertised a Grand Opening on Wednesday 8th November of that year, the film chosen being "The Game of Life" with Isobel Elsom. Vocalist Miss Irene Edwardes. The seating capacity was 841. The final curtain came on Saturday 13th Feburary 1965 with the showing of the films, "The Spy" (A) with Gerald Hatray and "Daggers Drawn" (A). It later opened as a Bingo and Leisure Centre. (below the interior which was rather grand).

Susan Peters

Pat O'Brian

Susanna Foster

The PICCADILLY SUPER CINEMA, 372-378 Stratford Road, Sparkbrook, Birmingham opened on the 22nd May 1930, proprietors The Hockley Picture House Co.Ltd., the film selected was "The Last of Mrs Cheyney" with Norma Shearer, Basil Rathbone, George Barraud and Hedda Hopper.   Seating capacity 2,050.   It was built adjacent to the site of the original Picturedrome which opened on the 26th December 1911 with a seating capacity of 700.   Prices of admission 6d and 1/-.   The fine Compton Organ installed was played by Harold Stringer.   For a number of years it published its own newspaper entitled "The Piccadilly Mirror".   From the 22nd April 1957 until it closed on the 2nd March 1974 it was under the management of L.D. Reeves.   The films chosen for the final performance being, "That'll Be The Day" (AA) with David Essex, Ringo Starr and Rosemary Leach and "The Man Who Haunted Himself" (A) with Roger Moore, Hildegarde Neil and Anton Rodgers.   It was then owned by the ABC Circuit and known as the ABC Sparkbrook.   For several years now it has been a Bingo and Social Club.

The PICCADILLY CINEMA, this re-opened on the 6th January 1995, it now has three auditoriums.

The PICTURE PLAYHOUSE, situated on the corner of Warwick and Station Road, Acocks Green, Birmingham opened in 1913 under the management of Ernest Brittain.   It had a seating capacity of 520.   Prices of admission from 2d to 1/-.   It was Licensed for Music.   It closed in 1929, one of the last films to be shown was, "Man, Woman and Sin", starring John Gilbert. It never went over to sound.

Maria Montez

The PICTUREDROME, Chapel Lane, Selly Oak, Birmingham, opened in 1913 under the management of T. Gathercole. In 1920 prices of admission were 6d and 1/-. It closed in the early 1920's when the Oak Cinema opened opposite.

"The PICTURE HOUSE, Witton Road, Witton, this was built by my Father in 1913. His name was William Capewell. He was quite a character and had many kinds of businesses (he and my Mother). In his early years he was a bandsman in the South Staffs., Regiment playing in Egypt in the war of 1880-81. The cinema was opened on September 13th 1913 which was my parents wedding anniversary. I was allowed to take two children every Saturday afternoon, one child was called Winnie Best whose auntie always gave us some sweets. I went to a Private School in Birchfield Road. My Father had all the school march down to the cinema and put on a special matinee for them, I proudly marched with them. You did not have tickets at the pay desk at that time. There were four prices of admission and a type of slot machine inside the pay desk which the attendant operated with her foot, it had four separate slots which issued the cheques outside the window. They were square pieces of metal with, diamond, spade, heart and club stamped out of the metal each denoting the price the customer paid. This was before the entertainment tax was put on, then normal tickets had to be issued".

Ena M. Parker

Note:—

In 1916 Mr Capewell re-named this cinema "The Empress", it had a seating capacity of 508. In 1936 the managing director was J.H. Herring, proprietors Suburban Halls Ltd. Entertainment Tax was first introduced by the Chancellor of the Exchequer in his 1916 budget.

June Allyson

Barbara Stanwyck

Phyllis Thayter

The PICTURE HOUSE, Ladypool Road, Sparkbrook, Birmingham, opened in 1915 under the management of E. Powell. In 1921 he was superseded by Harry Reubin when it changed its name to the New OLYMPIA Cinema. From 1945 to 1950 it was under the management of Mrs. J. Dawes. It had a seating capacity of 800. One of the directors was Mr. I.L. Lyons who was also a director of The Triangle, Bull Ring and Globe Cinemas. It closed in 1958.

Zasu Pitts

The PLAZA CINEMA, Stockland Green, Birmingham opened on Boxing Day 26th December 1927 under the management of William H. Denbigh. It had a seating capacity of 884. There was no official opening ceremony, the feature film chosen was, "The Cat and the Canary" starring Laura La Plante, the support film was "The Blond Saint", with Lewis Stone. Silent films were shown up to the 5th April 1930 and on the 7th April the first 'Talkie' was shown, "Sky Hawk" starring John Garrick. In 1933 the management was taken over by Frank Riego and he retained management until the cinema closed on the 30th September 1978, showing the films, "The Swarm" (A) with Michael Caine, Katharine Ross, Richard Widmark and Richard Chamberlain and "Good Old England", 45 years of unbroken service. The photograph was taken by Mr Riego's father on Sunday 19th June 1938 showing the long queue waiting to see the film, which commenced at 7.00 p.m. "When's Your Birthday" with Joe E. Brown.

Elvis Aaron Presley, the rock 'n' roll king. He is remembered for his early films, "King Creole", "Jail House Rock" and "G.I. Blues", these being only three of the 32 films he made up to 1971.

THE PLAZA
STOCKLAND GREEN, BIRMINGHAM.
Telephone: Erdington No. 1048.

Proprietors ... ... The Stockland Green Playhouse, Ltd.
Registered Offices, ... 43 Cannon Street, Birmingham.
Managing Director, ... George A. Parker, Esq.
Manager and Licensee, ... William H. Denbigh.
Chief Projectionist, ... William H. Alcock.

Continuous Performance Each Evening from 6.15,
excepting on SATURDAYS, when there will be TWO
SEPARATE PERFORMANCES, at 6.15 and 8.30. All Seats
bookable, 3d extra).
Matinees will be held at 2.45 p.m. each MONDAY,
WEDNESDAY, THURSDAY and SATURDAY.
Special Matinees will be held each Bank Holiday Tuesday
and on Boxing Day.

PRICES OF ADMISSION:
Balcony, 1/3. Stalls 9d and 6d.
Matinees—Balcony, 8d; Stalls, 4d.
NO HALF PRICES TO ANY PERFORMANCES.

Programmes are liable to Alteration through unforeseen
Circumstances.
The Management reserve the right to refuse Admission.
Outer Circle 'buses (No. 11) and Perry Common Cars
(No. 78) stop at the Theatre.
FREE CAR PARK FOR PATRONS.

If you would like a copy of this Programme each month
FREE OF CHARGE and POST FREE, please give your
name and address to the Cashier.

Name ....

Address, ...

This cinema was established in the Harborne Institute, Station Road, Harborne, Birmingham, in 1912, it was only operative for a few years.

Shani Wallis

Spencer Tracey

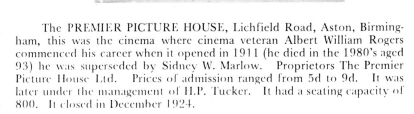

The PREMIER PICTURE HOUSE, Lichfield Road, Aston, Birmingham, this was the cinema where cinema veteran Albert William Rogers commenced his career when it opened in 1911 (he died in the 1980's aged 93) he was superseded by Sidney W. Marlow. Proprietors The Premier Picture House Ltd. Prices of admission ranged from 5d to 9d. It was later under the management of H.P. Tucker. It had a seating capacity of 800. It closed in December 1924.

The REGENT CINEMA, Ledsam Street, Ladywood, Birmingham opened in 1914 under the management of A.W. Withers, it was then known as the Ledsam Picture House. In 1930 it was re-named Regent and was then under the management of F.W. Robbins. It had a seating capacity of 700. Prices of admission ranged from 9d to 1/6, just prior to its closure in 1959 when this photograph was taken, the films shown were "Shack Out On 101", with Terry Moore, Frank Lovejoy and Lee Marvin, followed by "Tarzan Triumphs" with Johnny Weissmuller. At that time Ledsam Street was a thriving shopping centre and to the locals the cinema was always known as 'The Ledsam'.

Jennifer Jones

The REGAL CINEMA, 397 Soho Road, Handsworth, Birmingham was opened on Sunday 13th October 1929 by the Lord Mayor elect, Alderman M.L. Lancaster, J.P., it gave an outstanding programme of Vocal and Film Attractions including the B.B.C. Male Voice Choir. The Grand Compton Organ installed was played by H.A. Dowson. It had a seating capacity of 1,500 in the auditorium and 650 in the balcony. Prices of admission 6d and 1/6, reserved seats 2/-. Proceeds from this opening event were donated to local hospitals. When it closed on the 16th November 1968 it was known as Handsworth A.B.C., the film chosen was the three hour musical "Camelot" with Richard Harris and Vanessa Redgrave.

Audrey Totter

The ROYALTY CINEMA, High Street, Harborne, Birmingham opened on the 20th October 1930 showing the film, "The Love Parade" with Maurice Chevalier and Jeanette MacDonald. The manager was Patrick W. Campbell. Prices of admission 6d, 9d & 1/-. Proprietors Selly Oak Pictures Ltd. Seating capacity 1,500. It closed on Saturday the 2nd November 1963 with the showing of the films, "P.T.109" (U) with Cliff Robertson and Ty Hardin and "Bugs Bunny Show No 4" (U). It later opened as a Mecca Leisure Centre which is still operative today.

Walter Pidgeon

The RITZ CINEMA, 191 Bordesley Green East, Birmingham was opened on Monday 7th November 1927 by Sir Percival Bower, Kt. M.B.E., J.P., the films chosen were, "Nelson" and "The Triumph of the Rat". The Managing Director was W.M. Devey, Licensee and Manager Louis Lingard, musical director was Harold Jackson. It had a seating capacity of 1,442. It claimed to be the first cinema in the world to have Duo-Phantom Lighting System installed. The interior was majestic, as can be seen from the interior photograph hereunder. When it closed on Saturday 29th September 1962 it was under the management of L. Ward. Proprietors A.B.C. Circuit. Films chosen were, "The War of the Worlds" (X) with Gene Barry and Ann Robinson and "Detective Story" (X) with Kirk Douglas and Eleanor Parker. It later opened as the Ritz Bingo hall and is still operative, as such, today.

Greer Garson

Dame Flora Robson was created a C.B.E. in 1952 and a D.B.E. in 1960.

"The ROBIN HOOD, was a beautiful Cinema with a gold dome, inside were gold settees upholstered in red velvet, the passageways had tudor decor and over the screen was a huge handpainted scene depicting Robin Hood and his merry men. We used to go as children and wait outside asking people to take us in, so that we could see 'A' films because one had to be accompanied by an adult if it wasn't a 'U' film. In my courting days we went to the cinema three times a week.

Charges of admission were then 10d front stalls, 1/6d back stalls, 1/9d and 2/3d balcony. There was always a doorman to welcome you and the usherettes had smart uniforms with big bows on, they served ice cream cups from trays strapped around their necks." Memories from Mrs Joan N. Jones of Solihull.

The end of the Robin Hood in 1970, being surveyed sadly by the well known writer on the cinema in the 1950's, Leonard Rose.

The ROBIN HOOD CINEMA, situated on the corner of Stratford and Ingestre Road, Hall Green, Birmingham opened on Boxing Day, 26th December 1927, it was then known as the Robin Hood Theatre. The film chosen for the opening was "Ben-Hur", with Ramon Novarro playing the principal role and Francis X. Bushman as the villainous Messala. It had a seating capacity of 1,447. In 1936 it was managed by C.H. Putman, in 1943 S. Winterton and when it closed on the 7th March 1970, Arnold Lewis. The film chosen for this performance was "Zulu" (U), with Micahel Caine and Stanley Baker. Proprietors the ABC Circuit. It was later demolished to make way for a supermarket. (below depicts the interior which was impressive).

Mary Astor

The ROOKERY PICTURE PALACE, Rookery Road, Handsworth, Birmingham had a Grand Opening on Saturday 18th April 1914 the film selected "The White Witch". Prices of admission 3d & 6d children 2d & 3d. It had a seating capacity of 700. The proprietor was G.F. McDonald. A Miss Rosemary Savage, L.R.A.M., gave a piano solo at each evening performance. It was advertised as "The Coolest House in the Midlands". In 1920 it became the Headquarters of the Cinematograph Exhibitors Association of Great Britain and Ireland. In 1936 it was under the management of Chas. Williams who was previously the manager at the Futurist Cinema. It closed down on the 6th February 1957. The building has been used as a Religious Temple for a number of years now.

James Craig

The ROCK CINEMA, Alum Rock Road, Birmingham was opened on the 15th January 1934 by J.F. Eales, K.C. M.P. It had a seating capacity of 1,600. Prices of admission 7d, 9d & 1/-. It was built by C. Bryant & Son. Ltd., and the architect was Satchwell Roberts. The films chosen for this event were, "This Week of Grace" (U) and a Laurel & Hardy comedy. Music was provided by The Metropolitan Works Band. The manager was F.M. Hood. It closed on Sunday 16th January 1972 showing the film, "Phantom From 10,000 Leagues" (A).

Bebe Daniels

Ben Lyon

The RIALTO CINEMA, situated on the corner of Greenbank Avenue and Stratford Road, Hall Green, Birmingham opened on Monday 3rd October 1927 by Alderman Sir Percival Bower, Kt., M.B.E., J.P. The Licensee and manager was Joseph Drew. Seating capacity 960. The films chosen were, "Breakfast at Sunrise" with Constance Talmadge, and "Circus Life" with Marcella Albani. Proprietors Springfield Picture Playhouse Co. The orchestra was under the direction of W.E. Broadbent. Frederick Warrender and Foley Bates played the fine Compton Organ installed. In 1957 prices of admission ranged from 10d to 2/4d. Other managers were Joseph H. Rutter, Jack Harrison for 25 years and when it closed on the 30th May 1959 Cyril Riley. Films chosen for this sad event were "Black Orchid" (U) with Sophia Loren and Anthony Quinn and "When Hell Broke Loose" (U). A supermarket is now on this site.

"I was born in 1927, and the first film I saw was at the Rialto Cinema, and it starred Gracie Fields. I can't remember the title but I do remember my aunt trying to tease my fringe into a kiss curl such as Gracie had when we returned home. This was pre-school, but then from the time I was around six or seven, I used to go regularly. Mostly for a while with my father who used to work shifts but this meant that I was seeing mostly Westerns or jungle films. I suppose I was brain washed but I still enjoy these type of films today. When I was a little older I was allowed to go to the Saturday afternoon films and serials at the Tyseley Picture House which was just a few minutes away from my home at that time.

I fell in love with Larry (Buster) Crabbe as Flash Gordon, hated Emperor Ming, and hid my face when the Clay men were around. The Westerns were mostly starring Ken Maynard, or Gene Autry, but my favourite was Johnny Mack Brown, I couldn't stand Buck Jones.

Then I saw my first Tarzan film starring Johnny Weissmuller and from then on he was my hero. I saw all his films over and over and read all the Tarzan books, but when he was replaced in later years I never went to see any of the films. To me, he *was* Tarzan all the others were poor substitutes.

The Shirley Temple films were very popular, though I wasn't very keen on them, except the one called "Heidi" and I loved that one. Went to see it as often as it was on, not so much to see Shirley Temple, but I loved the old grandfather in the film. Jane Withers was always the hated girl in the Shirley Temple films a real nasty!

I never liked the George Formby films or the Laurel and Hardy ones though I did like the Marx Brothers, and Abbot and Costello. I liked the Will Hay films and especially Moore Marriot who played an old man in the films though I believe he wasn't all that old. I think that I saw every one of the Bing Crosby, Bob Hope Road pictures with Dorothy Lamour. I remember the term I left school, our teacher promised that she would take the class to the pictures if we did well in our exams. Well we did, and she took us to the Rialto to see the film "Moon over Burma" with Dorothy Lamour. We loved it, and I think at that time it was quite an unusual thing for a teacher to do, but we loved it.

The Deanna Durbin films were a must as well. I loved them all, especially "Three Smart Girls" and "Three Smart Girls Grow Up". One of the sisters in those films was Nan Grey who later married Frankie Laine, the singer.

67

The films in those days gave us our fashions, such as the Shirley Temple dresses, the Deanna Durbin hats, Lana Turner hair do's and Joan Crawfords square shouldered dresses and suits. My girl friend and I had Deanna Durbin hats and did our hair the same as she did, then we copied Betty Grables hair do. Our lives were very much influenced by the films and the stars at that time.

During my teen years I loved the musicals. Mickey Rooney growing up after the Andy Hardy films, Judy Garland, "Meet Me in St. Louis" being a particular favourite. Saw all the Betty Grable films, mostly musicals, all colourful, and romantic Don Ameche was usually around and Carmen Miranda too. Sheer escapism. Rita Hayworth was another favourite whose hair styles we tried to copy with our strong setting lotion and "dinkie" steel curlers . . . such torture.

Victor Mature was a special favourite. I especially enjoyed seeing him in a muscial called "My Gal Sal" and later, I saw "Samson and Delilah" and "The Robe", over and over. I remember his getting engaged to Rita Hayworth. He was in the U.S. Coastguard service at the time. She jilted him and married Orson Welles and I can remember shedding a few tears when I read in a film magazine the headlines, "Has Rita Broken Vic's Heart". Looking back it seems so stupid to be so affected, but I think we knew so much about the stars then and became so involved that they were like people we had known for years.

Regarding cinema attendances, it was possible to go every day if one wanted because every cinema showed something different. My nearest Cinema was the Tyseley, but only a short distance away was the Piccadilly, the Warwick and the Rialto. I used to like the interior of the Warwick depicting as it did, Warwick Castle, but I liked the organist at the Piccadilly, and after I met my then future husband, the Piccadilly was the cinema we went to the most. I used to enjoy though, going to the cinemas in the city, especially the Paramount (now the Odeon) with its impressive decor and the tea room. I liked the West End cinema too. Looking back it amazes me how we stood in those long queues so patiently, waiting and hoping for a seat.

A few of my favourite films were "Waterloo Bridge" — Robert Taylor and Vivien Leigh, "Mrs Miniver" — Greer Garson and Walter Pidgeon, "Goodbye Mr. Chips" also Greer Garson with Robert Donat. "Way to the Stars" Michael Redgrave and John Mills, "State Fair" — Jeanne Craine and Dick Haymes, "You Came Along" with Liz Scott and Robert Cummings, "Song of Bernadette" with Jennifer Jones and "The Third Man" with Orson Welles.

The forties were the golden years of the cinema for me. Not I suppose because the films were all that good, though we all thought that they were at the time, mostly because going to the cinema was such a large part of our life then.

Mrs Hazel Smith
Solihull

Ann Todd

A still from the film, "Bridge on the River Kwai" made in 1957 and voted the best film of the year, starring Alec Guinness, William Holden and Jack Hawkins. Directed by David Lean, it was awarded 7 Academy Awards. It was made in Technicolor and ran for 2 hours 41 minutes.

Gordon Jackson

The SALTLEY PICTURE PALACE, 20 Alum Rock Road, Saltley, Birmingham opened on the 3rd July 1911, under the management of Bert Sharp. Architect Harry H. Reynolds. Prices of admission 6d, 4d & 2d. In 1915 the manager was Harry Hampton, a former Aston Villa Football Club centre forward and an international player. In 1921 it was managed by T. Churchman. In the 1930's it held Sunday Concerts and gave the proceeds to charity. It closed in the 1960's but re-opened on the 6th October 1979, the matinee performance was free to children, the evening performance screened the film, "Saturday Night Fever" (A) with John Travolta and Karen Lynn Gorney. It closed in December 1983, when it was known as The Palace Cinema, under the management of A.S. Bains, an application for the renewal of the Cinematograph Licence was refused on the grounds that the premises did not meet the safety and hygiene requirement laid down by the licencing authority. In November 1984 it opened as The Saltley Supermarket.

Billie Burke, the actress with the pleasant voice. Remember her with Judy Garland in the film "The Wizard of Oz" made in 1939.

The SELLY OAK PICTUREDROME, People's Hall, Oak Tree Lane, Selly Oak, Birmingham. Gave performances twice nightly 7 & 9 p.m. Childrens matinees on Saturdays at 2.00 and 3.30 p.m. admission 1d. Opened in 1911 closed a few years later.

SPARKHILL PICTURE PALACE, this picture was taken shortly after the cinema opened, it shows a very young Mr Sydney H. Last, who was employed there and who, eventually went to manage the Victoria and Coronet Cinemas in Small Heath, he was later appointed manager at the Sheldon Cinema when it opened in 1937.

The SAVOY CINEMA, 883 Stratford Road, Sparkhill, Birmingham, opened in 1911 when it was known as The Sparkhill Picture Palace. Proprietors The Hockley Picture House Co.Ltd., It was under the management of Mrs Bert Wallace, she was superseded by W.E. Steven. It had a seating capacity of 570. From 1918 to 1925 it was under the management of E.N. Belsten, prices of admission then being 6d, 9d and 1/-. When the Charlie Chaplin film, "Shoulder Arms" was presented the manager had a model of a first world war dug-out built in the foyer to promote the film. It had a very good orchestra, the first violinist being Frank Cantell, he had a small electric light fitted on the end of his violin bow as a novelty. The cinema had its own gas engined generator as a source of electricity, this was housed in a shed at the rear of the property, one day, the huge flywheel slid off its spindle, crashed through the shed, careered down Nansen Road, over Stratford Road and finished up in a florists window, fortunately no-one was injured. The cinema never went over to sound and closed in 1930, it was a billiard hall for some time but in recent years it has been a motor car showroom.

The SHELDON

THE MANAGEMENT

Mr. Sydney H. Last.

The Directors have every confidence in appointing Mr. Sydney H. Last to the Management of "The Sheldon." His vast experience of the Trade extends over twenty-nine years, for he started his cinematic career in 1908, as an operator—now known as a "projectionist."

Incidentally he was the first man in Birmingham to show the film of the Coronation of King George V. in 1911 (he could tell you a fine story about that great event!)

He was appointed Manager of "The Coronet" in 1930 and has steadily built up an enviable reputation for courtesy and friendliness amongst the patrons of that Theatre.

As Manager of "The Sheldon" he will be pleased at all times to consider any suggestions for the betterment of your comfort, or entertainment, that may be forthcoming.

In addition, a specially selected staff has been engaged to ensure that everything will be done to make your visits here something to look forward to each week.

FOR YOUR INFORMATION
PERFORMANCES

MATINEES DAILY (EXCEPT FRIDAY) AT 2-45.	DOORS OPEN AT 2-15 p.m.
EVENINGS CONTINUOUS FROM 6-0 p.m.	DOORS OPEN AT 5-40 p.m.
SUNDAYS AT 7-0 p.m.	DOORS OPEN AT 6-20 p.m.

PRICES OF ADMISSION
(Including Tax)
MATINEES (Holidays excepted)

ALL STALLS - - - 4d.	CIRCLE - - - 6d.	BALCONY - - - 6d.
Children - - - - 3d.	Children - - - 4d.	Children - - - 4d.

EVENINGS

FRONT STALLS - 6d.	REAR STALLS - 9d.	BALCONY - 1/-	CIRCLE - 1/3
Children - - 4d.	Children - 4d.	Children - 6d.	Children - 6d.

No Reduced Prices for Children on Saturdays, Sundays, Mondays and Holidays.

SPACIOUS **FREE CAR PARK** FOR USE OF PATRONS AT OWNERS' RISK.

TELEPHONE - SHELDON 2158.

The SHELDON CINEMA, Coventry Road, Birmingham, opened on the 10th October 1937 under the management of Sydney H. Last. The film chosen was, "Three Smart Girls" (A) (see copy programme). It had a seating capacity of 1467. In 1957 prices of admission ranged from 1/- to 2/9, during this period, when the film, "The Day The Earth Stood Still" was shown, starring Michael Rennie, Patricia Neal and Hugh Marlowe, the manager had a 10ft high model of a Robot displayed in the foyer to promote the film. It closed on the 26th November 1977 with the films, "Orca-Killer Whale" (A) with Richard Harris and Charlotte Rampling. The 'B' film was "Holiday on the Buses" (A). L.A. Gibbons was the manager.

The last two patrons at the Cinema on the 26th November 1977, the attractive cashier is Mrs K. Beale.

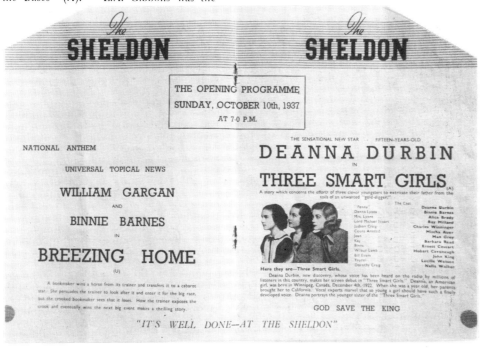

71

The SAVOY CINEMA, 1649-1651, Pershore Road, Stirchley, Birmingham opened on the 27th February 1933 after the premises had been refurbished and modernised.   The films chosen were, "Tenderfoot" and "Working Wives".   Prices of admission 6d & 9d stalls, 1/- & 1/3 circle.   It was then known as "The Palace Cinema".   Prior to opening it was a theatre and music hall known as the Kings Norton Palace of Varieties.   The resident pianist was Reg. Shaw.   It closed on the 2nd February 1958 with the film "Womans Prison".   One of the early managers was Miss Lilian M. Jenner, she was appointed at the age of 22 years, she had control of a staff of 18.   Her appointment was unique in the Midlands, she left school at the age of 14, became a cinema attendant and from then on, owing to her ability was given this position.   Her favourite film was, "Smilin Through", made in 1932.   This was a record breaking film starring Norma Shearer, Leslie Howard, Ralph Forbes and Frederic March.

The SPRINGFIELD CINEMA, Stratford Road, Springfield, Birmingham, opened in 1915 when it was known as The Springfield Picture Playhouse and under the management of Harry Dewey.   It had a seating capacity of 600.   He retired on the 31st March 1922, his daughter Dorothy was the pianist in those silent days.   It closed on Saturday 31st May 1958 showing the films, "Davy" (U) with Harry Secombe and "The Hired Hand" (U) with Rory Calhoun.   The photograph on the left was taken at the entrance to the cinema in 1950, from left to right Arthur Hinton the 2nd operator, Johnny Owens and A.T. Lee the Chief Operator.

72

Original building 1914

After a face lift 1955

The STAR PICTURE HOUSE, Slade Road, Erdington, Birmingham. When it opened in 1914 it was known as The Gravelly Hill Picture House and was under the able management of E. Russell Yeulett. Proprietors Gravelly Hill Picture House Ltd. Prices of admission 3d, 4d & 6d. Seating capacity 1,000. One of the first films to be shown was on Saturday 6th June 1914, "Black Mafia". In 1915 it was managed by H.J. Smithers and in 1943 Mrs E. Keppey. It was later purchased by William Devey who had other cinema interests in the Birmingham area. From 1946 to 30th August 1958, when it closed, it was managed by W.A. James. The films chosen for this performance were "Pal Joey" (U) with Frank Sinatra and Rita Hayworth, the 'B' film was "Parson and the Outlaw" (U) with Anthony Dexter. In 1949 Professor Jimmy Edwards, Joyce Golding and Freddy Frinton, who were appearing at the Birmingham Hippodrome, took time off to visit 'The Star' to see a film, "Trouble in the Air", apparently they had all appeared in this film but had never had the opportunity to see it before. A good time was had by all. The building was derelict for several years before it was finally demolished in 1981.

THE STAR PICTURE PALACE,

SLADE ROAD, GRAVELLY HILL.

Manager   · · ·   1914 ·   E RUSSELL YEULETT.

A PICTURE HOUSE APART FROM ALL OTHERS.

Continuous Performances, 6-30 to 10-30.

MATINEE   ·   Wednesday & Saturday at 3 p.m.

ADMISSION :—3d., 4d., 6d.

CAFE LOUNGE   ·   NINEPENCE.

A Combination of Pleasures——Take your Refreshments while viewing the Pictures.

STIRCHLEY EMPIRE

Pershore Road   Phone Kin 1663

To-day and To-morrow,

DOUGLAS FAIRBANKS Jr. and NANCY CARROLL in

SCARLET DAWN (A) also

Interest—**Beneath the Sea**

SERIAL—LOST SPECIAL Episode 12

Monday, June 19th

LEE TRACEY in

Half Naked Truth (U)

A Million laugh power Romance

Also—DOROTHY REVIER in

A SCARLET WEEK END (A)

Thursday, June 22nd

PAUL MUNI in

I AM A FUGITIVE (A)

and full Supporting Programme

MATINEES - Mondays, Wednesdays, Thursdays, and Saturdays at 2-30 p.m.

The STIRCHLEY EMPIRE, 1250 Pershore Road, Stirchley, Birmingham opened by Cuthbert Morrall in 1912. In 1936 it was under the management of F.A. Dawson. When the film, "Shanghai Express", which was made in 1932 starring Marlene Dietrich, Clive Brook and Anna May Wong, was shown, the manager transformed the foyer, as a gimmick, into a railway booking office and distributed tickets for the 'Shanghai Express' he also had a large cut-out of a train attached to the wall of a nearby garage to help promote the film. The advertisement displayed appeared in the local press on the 16th June 1933. The cinema closed circa 1950.

The STIRCHLEY PAVILION, Pershore Road, Stirchley, Birmingham was opened on Saturday 28th November 1931 by Sir Percival Bower, Kt. M.B.E., J.P. The film chosen was "Cimarron" with Richard Dix and Irene Dunne and a cast of 40,000. Seating capacity 2,500. It had a fine Christie Organ installed. When the film "Angels One Five" was shown in the early 1950's, starring Jack Hawkins, John Gregson and Michael Dennison, a Hurricane Aircraft from the Second World War was put on display on the forecourt to promote the film. In 1954 it was under the management of P. Freedman. In 1960 it underwent extensive alterations and was converted into a Bowling Alley and Cinema known as the A.B.C. Cine-Bowl. Closure came on Saturday 27th December 1968 with the showing of the films, "The Belles of St. Trinians" (U) with Alastair Sim, George Cole and Joyce Grenfell, the 'B' film chosen was "Raising a Riot" (U). Further alterations were made and it opened as a Bingo and Bowl venue called 'The Star'.

The TIVOLI CINEMA, Coventry Road, South Yardley, Birmingham opened on 17th October 1927 with the film "Beyond the Rocks" with Rudolph Valentino and Gloria Swanson. The first manager, who served for 20 years, was Percy Thompson, he was superseded by Ernest Edge. In its 'silent' days it had a fine orchestra directed by Louis Benson. It had a seating capacity of 1,300. It gave its last performance on Saturday 1st July 1961 and the feature film chosen was "Facts of Life" (A) with Bob Hope, Lucille Ball and Ruth Hussey. It was demolished and a supermarket complex erected on the site.

The TEMPERANCE HALL, Temple Street, Birmingham was originally a concert hall but showed Kinemacolor Animated Pictures in July 1910. It showed normal films in 1921 when it was under the management of J.H. Lear Hall. It had a seating capacity of 900.

TEMPERANCE HALL
TEMPLE STREET, BIRMINGHAM.

BIRMINGHAM AUDIENCES DELIGHTED WITH
The Greatest Invention of the Century.

KINEMACOLOR
Animated Pictures
IN ALL THE ACTUAL.
Hues & Tints of Nature

Afternoon Performances at 3 and 4 p.m.
Evening (Continuous) 6 to 10 p.m.
Admission - 1/-, 6d. & 3d.

The TUDOR CINEMA, Haunch Lane, Kings Heath, Birmingham, opened on the 30th March 1929 by Alderman A.H. James accompanied by Sir Percival and Lady Bower, it was under the management of Albert H. Harrison, seating capacity 1,000. A Grand Star Programme was arranged. The architect was Harold S. Scott, builders W.T. Whittall & Son Ltd. Proprietors Tudor Picture House Co.Ltd. Closure came on Saturday 17th March 1962 with the showing of the films, "Petticoat Pirates" (U) with Charlie Drake and "Drums for a Queen" (U). It has been for a number of years now a Social Centre and Bingo Club.

The TRIANGLE CINEMA, Gooch Street, Balsall Heath, Birmingham opened on the 8th October 1923 with the films, "The Pilgrim" with Charlie Chaplin and "The Yellow Stain" with John Gilbert plus "Felix the Cat". The Manager was Jack Walker. It had a seating capacity of 606. Prices of admission 3d, 5d and 9d children half price. It was built on the site of Pringles Palace which was originally erected in 1913. In 1959 it became the Headquarters of the Asian Film Industry in Birmingham.

The TYSELEY CINEMA, Warwick Road, Greet, Birmingham, opened in 1915, proprietors S & E Cinemas Ltd., and County Cinemas Ltd. Seating capacity 912. In 1921 it was under the management of Percy Dyche, prices of admission ranged from 5d to 1/-. It closed on Sunday 29th November 1959 showing the film "Six Bridges to Cross" with Tony Curtis and George Nader.

The VICTORIA PICTURE HOUSE, 594 Coventry Road, Small Heath, Birmingham opened in 1912 under the management of Mrs Sheila Hyde, she was followed by J.W. Atkinson. Sidney H. Last was manager for several years but when it closed on the 18th April 1931, showing the film "If Business Interferes" it was managed by A. Whitworth Cheetham. Popular serials were a feature of this cinema which included "Blake of Scotland Yard" and "The Pirate of Panama".

The VICTORIA PLAYHOUSE, 320 Victoria Road, Aston, Birmingham opened on the 16th December 1924, the film chosen was "Cornered" considered a classic at that time. Selected music and Orchestral arrangements were by R. Arthur Jones, (who had previously been at West's Picture House, in Erdington). Architect H.W.W. Lovegrove. Seating capacity 1,300. Prices of admission in the 1950's 1/- to 2/2. Proprietor A.W. Rogers. It was later taken over by Victoria Playhouse (B'ham)Ltd. It closed on Saturday 3rd August 1963, films selected being "Ursus in the Valley of the Lions" (U) and "Where The River Bends" (U).

Lilian Gish

Before and After

The VILLA CROSS PICTURE HOUSE, Heathfield Road, Handsworth, Birmingham, opened in 1915 when it was known as the New Picture House. It was opened by Irving Bosco who later founded the company, Bosco's Picture Ltd., in 1920 it was under the management of W. Wilmot-Carlton, prices of admission ranged from 5d to 1/3. Seating capacity 1,500. In 1924 Raymond De Courcy and his Orchestra moved there from the Delicia Cinema. From 1932 to 1941 it was under the management of Mr Bowgen. Proprietors Rank Organisation. It closed on the 20th April 1970 with the showing of the film, "Ice Star to Zebra" with Rock Hudson, Ernest Borgnine and Patrick McGoohan. For a number of years now it has been a Bingo and Social Club. It was built on the site of Shorts Carriage Works, who ran a carriage hire business run by Mr Short Snr., and his four sons. The premises housed 37 horses and 12 carriages.

Ben Turpin

W.C. Fields

The WALDORF PICTURE THEATRE, Walford Road, Sparkbrook, Birmingham opened, without ceremony, in 1913, the first advertisement appeared in the local press on Wednesday 24th December of that year when it was under the management of J.W. Atkinson. It had a seating capacity of 820 and had an all Ladies Orchestra as a special attraction. It closed in 1950 for refurbishment and re-opened on 10th April with the film "New Adventures of Don Juan" with Errol Flynn and Viceca Lindfors. It terminated its licence to give public performances, when it was under the management of A.S. Randhawa, on the 18th November 1981 as it was proposed to turn the premises into a members only club.

Harry Langdon

Zsa Zsa Gabor

Rosalind Russell

Souvenir Programme

OF THE OPENING OF

THE

" WARWICK "

SUPER CINEMA

ACOCKS GREEN.

MONDAY, SEPTEMBER 16, 1929.

The WARWICK CINEMA, Westley Road, Acocks Green, Birmingham was opened on the 16th September 1929 by E. Hewitson presided over by S.W.B. Stephen. Films selected being "Happiness Ahead" with Colleen Moore and "Riley the Cop" with Farrell Macdonald and Louise Fazenda. Music was provided by the Warwick Orchestra under the direction of Noel Wimperis with selections from "Chu Chin Chow". Seating capacity 1,300. Prices of admission Circle 1/2. Stalls 6d. In 1936 it was under the management of P. Douglas Reeves, the above photograph was taken during his term of management. It closed in 1962 for modernisation and rebuilding into a cinema and bowling alley, the cinema portion was not opened until 29th March 1964, film chosen being "Father Came Too" (A) with Stanley Baker and James Robertson Justice. Seating capacity 462. Manager L. Shiels. The present manager is Chris. Bryan and the proprietors The Victoria Playhouse Group.

The WEOLEY CINEMA, Barnes Hill, Weoley Castle, Birmingham opened on Saturday 1st August 1936 by the Weoley Castle Carnival Queen. The film selected, "Captain Blood" with Errol Flynn and Olivia de Haviland. The Architect was H.W. Way Lovegrove. It had a seating capacity of 850. All proceeds from this opening performance were given to charity. It closed on Saturday 30th September 1961 films selected "The Magnificent Seven" (U) with Yul Brynner and Steve McQueen and "The Police Dog Story" (U) with James Brown. It was later demolished.

The WINSON GREEN PICTURE HOUSE, corner of Winson Green Road and Wellington Road, Winson Green, Birmingham opened in 1914 and was under the management of Harry Devey. It had a seating capacity of 1,400. It closed on Saturday 21st March 1959 showing the films, "Sea of Sand" (U) with Richard Attenborough and "Suspended Alibi" (U).

RIN-TIN-TIN, the dog star who appeared in over 50 films, his greatest being "A Dog of the Regiment", based on his own life, how he was discovered in the German trenches in the First World War after saving the life of Lieut. Lee Duncan of the US army (depicted in the photograph), who, afterwards became his owner and trainer. He died aged 16 years on the 10th August 1932.

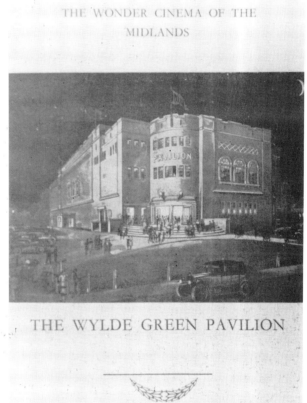

THE WONDER CINEMA OF THE
MIDLANDS

THE WYLDE GREEN PAVILION

The WYLDE GREEN PAVILION, situated on the corner of Gravelly Lane and Chester Road, Wylde Green, Birmingham, was opened on the 10th October 1931 by the Mayoress of Sutton Coldfield, Mrs Joseph A. Oldbury (see copy programme for full details). The Architect was Harold S. Scott and the building contractors G.T. Stephens & Son. It had a seating capacity of 2,184. The Directors were Sir Percival Bower, Kt. M.B.E., Chairman. Joseph Cohen & Harold S. Scott were joint managing directors. Walter B Bond; William E. Wright; A.J. Lloyd and J.S. Bruce. The General Manager was F. Stephen Sandover. An organ recital was given by Frank Matthews on the first Christin Organ Unit to be installed in a Birmingham Cinema. The decoration of the interior was an artistic joy and appealed to all lovers of beauty. It finally closed on Saturday 3rd September 1960 showing the films, "Sands of the Desert" (U) with Charlie Drake and Peter Arne and "Raymie" (U) with David Ladd. The building was later converted into a Bowling Alley but this proved not to be successful and it was demolished in the 1970's.

F 281

CITY OF
BIRMINGHAM
TO WIT

A T a Petty Sessions of Her Majesty's Justices of the Peace, of and for the City of Birmingham, holden in and for the said City, at the Victoria Law Courts, in Corporation Street, in the said City, on the   6th   day of   October,   19 52

The Justices of the Peace acting for the said City present at this Petty Sessions, in pursuance of the powers delegated to them by the Lord Mayor, Aldermen, and Citizens of the said City acting by the Council of the said City, by virtue of " The Cinematograph Acts, 1909 and 1952," hereby grant to Ronald Baden Voyce
(hereinafter called the licensee) this licence to use certain premises situate at   Bristol Road South, Northfield

in the said City, and known as the   Northfield Cinema

for cinematograph exhibitions on every day except Sundays, Christmas Day and any day appointed for a public fast or thanksgiving, between the hours of 12 noon and 11 p.m.

The licensee shall observe and keep all the Regulations made by the Secretary of State for the time being in force relating to such exhibitions as aforesaid.

This licence will be suspended by the Justices in the event of any failure on the part of the licensee to carry out the said Regulations, or of the building becoming otherwise unsafe, or of any material alteration being made in the building or enclosure without the consent of the Justices.

This licence is granted upon and subject to : —

(a) The terms, conditions and restrictions set out in the Regulations annexed hereto (but excepting such Regulations as are stated not to apply to this licence).

(b) Any undertaking that may have been given to the Justices.

(c) The additional condition, so far as Good Friday is concerned, that any entertainment given on that day shall be in every respect appropriate and suitable to the day.

This licence shall, unless revoked or suspended in the meantime, be in force for one year from the fifth day of December next.

Given under the Official Stamp of the Justices, which is hereto affixed under their authority, by me.

Cinematograph Licence.—F.

FEE—One Year, £1
For every Month, 5 -
(Aggregate payable in any year not to exceed £1)

Amount paid   £1

Clerk to the Justices

82

This firm were cinematograph machine makers
and distributors period 1912—1914.

This is the type of still that was hired to cinema managers, by Wardour
Films, in the silent film era.   Note the wooden bracket that is holding
up the set on the right of the picture.

"Susannah of the Mounties" made in 1939.

Clark Gable and Vivien Leigh
in the 1939 film, "Gone with the Wind".

CELLULOID HOOFBEATS

Buffalo Bill was the first man to present the Cowboy and the Indian to the people of Birmingham when he played here in 1887, and later at Perry Barr in June 1903.

The same year the first Western with a story was made, "The Great Train Robbery", and the public wanted more of this type of picture. G.M. Anderson a bit player in this one reeler moved out to California and after a few Westerns starred in the "Broncho Billy" series, the Western hero was born.

Cowboys flocked to Hollywood in their hundreds to earn more money in a week than they could in a month on a ranch. Many were Rodeo Champions, some ex-lawmen and a few were outlaws. It was the last outpost of the Old West.

Early Western players like Tex McLeod (later a great favourite spinning his ropes and yarns at the Grand, Empire and Hippodrome) Hoot Gibson, Art Acord, Jack Hoxie, contested in Rodeos during the summer and did picture work in the winter months.

One of the early Cowboy stars to appear on stage in the City was young Buffalo, (Philip Yale Drew) when he played at the Metropole in "King of the Wild West", with his horse Major in October 1910.

For the first twenty-five years the gunfire and hoofbeats were silent and the big names were Harry Carey, William S. Hart, Art Acord, Hoot Gibson, Buck Jones, Ken Maynard, Tim McCoy, and the flamboyant Tom Mix. Tom was the most famous and highest paid of them all, he first came to Birmingham in 1925 with the original horse Tony. His great horse was stabled at Cave's Horse Repository in Moseley Street and Tom exercised him early each morning in Queen's Ride in Cannon Hill Park.

Eddie Polo the great serial star came over the same year as Tom and played a week at the Empire in his show, "The Golden West". My father saw both and often spoke of what was a highlight for him.

As the 1920's drew to a close Talking Pictures opened up a whole new scene for the public. Two Cowboys managed two firsts in this field. Tex McLeod was the first Cowboy to talk in pictures when he made "Tex McLeod in a Rope and a Story", for Warner Brothers in 1928, and Ken Maynard was the first singing Cowboy in Universals "Wagon - master" in 1929.

Through the 1930's all the cinemas across Birmingham echoed to the sound of gunfire. Buck Jones and Silver were the most beloved of them all, managers rubbed their hands as the kids flocked to see their heroes.

In September 1938 Tom Mix came to Birmingham again for a week at the Hippodrome. This time I was fortunate enough to see him when my mother took me to New Street Station. To see him with his white horse Tony II was a moment I have never forgotten.

The following year I saw Gene Autry on Champion, again at New Street Station. It was another great event in my young life, and to see them in the flesh when I had only seen them on the screen was the stuff dreams were made of.

No Hollywood Cowboys came over to perform during the war years but Tex McLeod was still on hand at the Hippodrome and the Windsor with his horses and rope tricks.

During March of 1954 I saw Roy Rogers at the Hippodrome with Dale Evans and his beautiful Palomino horse Trigger. Roy, like Tom Mix, stayed at the Queen's Hotel and Trigger signed the hotel register with a pencil between his teeth.

Fess Parker of Davie Crocket fame, both on large and small screens paid a visit to Lewis's Store in 1956. So many children and adults turned up that the manager had to close the store.

May of 1973 saw another great singing cowboy, Tex Ritter, playing for a one night stand in Erdington. The place was packed and many fans were calling for him to sing songs from movies he had made 35 years earlier. I spent an hour and a half with him and met his wife the former Dorothy Fay who, in earlier years, had been rescued from the Villains on our screens by the likes of Buck Jones, Bob Baker and Tex Ritter himself.

Now ten years on, the Celluloid Hoofbeats are silent once again as are the cinemas the old cowboys battled in week after week. No heroes, no cinemas to speak of, it just doesn't seem possible. But at least we have our memories of those we saw on the screen and the ones some of us were lucky enough to see in the flesh.

John M. Hall

TOM MIX — born 6th January 1880 at Mix Run, Pennsylvania, U.S.A. He was a real cowboy who wanted, and succeeded in becoming a Western Star. He not only starred in such films as "Five Thousand Dollar Reward", "Horseman of the Plain" and "Destry Rides Again", but also directed films. He had a magic and flamboyant personality. When he visited London in the twenties he galloped daily in Hyde Park clad in his most elaborate cowboy outfit, and rode up the steps of the Mansion House on his famous horse Tony. When in Birmingham he exercised his horse daily in Queens Ride, in Cannon Hill Park.

HARRY CAREY — born in the Bronx area of New York on the 16th January 1878 son of a New York Judge, he died, after being bitten by a black widow spider on the 21st September 1947 in California. His first film was "Bill Sharkey's Last Game", made in 1910, he was also in the epic film "Trader Horn" made in 1931 by M.G.M. His last film, released in 1948 was "Red River" starring John Wayne, his son Harry Carey Jnr was also in this film.

ROY ROGERS — the popular singing cowboy with is wife and partner on the silver screen, Dale Evans. His now famous Palomino Horse, Trigger, who starred with him in 87 films and over 100 T.V. shows, died on the 3rd July 1965 in Los Angeles, he was 31 years of age and billed as 'the smartest horse in the movies!' He received 1,000 fan letters a week.

REX ALLEN — the last of the singing cowboys. Born in Willcox, Arizona on the 31st December 1921, with his horse 'Koko'. His first film was "The Arizona Cowboy" in 1950 and his last film "The Phantom Stallions" in 1954.

GENE AUTRY — one of the most popular singing cowboys with his equally popular horse Champion. Born in Tiogo, Texas on the 29th September 1907. His first film was "In Old Santafe" in 1934 and his last film was "Last of the Pony Riders" in 1953.

CINEMATOGRAPH ACTS 1909 AND 1952

Consent for Cinematograph Exhibitions for Children

AT A PETTY SESSIONS of Her Majesty's Justices of the Peace of and for the City of Birmingham, holden in and for the said City, at the Victoria Law Courts in Corporation Street in the said City, on the 16th day of October, 1953 .

THE JUSTICES OF THE PEACE acting for the said City, present at this Petty Sessions, in pursuance of the powers delegated to them by the Lord Mayor. Aldermen and Citizens of the said City acting by the Council of the said City, by virtue of the above-mentioned Acts, hereby consent to the use by

Ronald Baden Voyce
(hereinafter called "the licensee") of certain premises situate at

Bristol Road South, Northfield
in the said City and known as the   Northfield Cinema
for cinematograph exhibitions for children on every Saturday

(except any day appointed for a public fast or thanksgiving), for one year from the fifth day of December next, subject to the conditions and restrictions set out below :

1. Any such exhibition shall be given between the hours of 10 a.m. and 12 noon, and/or between the hours of 1.30 p.m. and 4 p.m.

2. The licensee shall observe and keep all the regulations for the time being in force made by the Secretary of State in pursuance of the Cinematograph Acts, 1909 and 1952 relating to such exhibitions.

3. This consent is granted upon and subject to the terms conditions and restrictions set out in the regulations annexed to the licence of the said premises relating to cinematograph exhibitions in general.

4. No child shall be permitted to be in the two front rows of the balcony unless the child is accompanied by and in the charge of a person who appears to have attained the age of 16 years.

5. This consent is liable to be withdrawn in the event of any contravention of the foregoing or of any other conditions and restrictions subject to which the said premises are allowed to be used for cinematograph exhibitions for children.

GIVEN under the Official Stamp of the Justices, which is hereto affixed under their authority by me.

F. D. [signature]

Clerk to the Justices.

CONSENT
CINEMATOGRAPH EXHIBITIONS FOR CHILDREN

FEE 5/-
250 4.7.55

Jack Wild

ASK A POLICEMAN.

"CAN YOU RECOMMEND SOME NICE PICTURES FOR NICE CHILDREN?"

[A deputation from the Birmingham Cinema Enquiry Committee was yesterday received by the Home Secretary, who was asked to take steps to improve the general standard of films, especially those exhibited to children.]

Mark Lester

Deanna Dubrin

Judy Garland

Margaret O'Brien

'OUR GANG' who gave us so many laughs was originally produced by Hal Roach in 1922 with Mickey Daniels, Sunshine Sammy, Jackie Gordon, Fat Joe Cobb, Farina & Mary Kornman. As they outgrew their roles others were enrolled into the gang, Johnny Down, Jean Darling, 'Stymie' and Jackie Cooper. Remember their dog 'Pete'? They were later re-named 'The Little Rascals'.

Walter Disney was born in Chicago, Illinois, U.S.A. on the 5th December 1901. He served as an ambulance driver with the Red Cross in France during the First World War.

In 1928, after working in the Film Industry in America, he developed the cartoon series that introduced Mickey Mouse in "Steamboat Willie", the first cartoon film made with sound, later he introduced Minnie Mouse, Mickey's sweetheart.

This was the beginning of the Disney Films as we know them, later came Pluto, Donald Duck and the films we all loved and still see from time to time on T.V. today.

In 1932 he released the film "Flowers and Trees" and won an Academy Award, then followed the "Silly Symphony" series. In 1937 we saw the films "Snow White and the Seven Dwarfs", 1940 — "Pinocchio" and "Fantasia". In 1941 "Dumbo", 1948 "Seal Island", and "The Living Desert", which proved to be the biggest ever money maker film. 1950 "Cinderella", 1951 "Alice in Wonderland", 1953 "Peter Pan", 1954 "The Wonderful World of Disney", 1955 "Lady and The Tramp", in this year DISNEYLAND was opened in Anaheim, California. Then came the films "The Vanishing Prairie" and "The African Lion".

From the Walt Disney film,
"Alice in Wonderland" made by Paramount in 1933.

Mickey Mouse

Donald Duck & Pluto

GEORGE ARLISS — English gentleman actor who was seldom seen on the British stage made all his films in Hollywood, his acting ability endeared him to millions of fans. Starred in many films such as "Disraeli", "Voltaire", "The Green Goddess" and "House of Rothschild".

RONALD REAGAN — Born 6th February 1912 in Tampicom, Illinois, U.S.A. He was never a 'Star' but made numerous films including "The Hasty Heart", Bedtime for Bonzo", "The Last Outpost", "Law and Order" and "Tennessee's Partner". He was elected the 40th President of the United States of America on the 4th November, 1980.

WILLIAM POWELL, well known actor and a ladies man. First played the part of Lt. Trench in the last of the big silent films in 1929 but best known for his portrayal of Nick Charles, the detective, in the 'Thin Man' series in 1936. He made, with Myrna Loy, six films in this series, one must not forget the dog 'Asta'. He was married to Carole Lombard another well known actress at that period. He starred in the film "The Great Ziegfeld" in 1936 and the film won an Oscar.

William Powell

CASABLANCA a 4 star Hollywood film made in 1942 with romance intrigue, excitement and suspense and a little humour.

Myrna Loy

SUNDAY ENTERTAINMENTS ACT, 1932
PERMIT FOR CINEMATOGRAPH ENTERTAINMENTS ON SUNDAYS.

AT A PETTY SESSIONS *of Her Majesty's Justices of the Peace of and for the City of Birmingham, holden in and for the said City, at the Victoria Law Courts in Corporation Street in the said City, on Monday the fifteenth day of December 1958.*

THE JUSTICES OF THE PEACE acting for the said City, present at this Petty Sessions, in pursuance of their powers under the above-mentioned Act and every other power enabling them, DO HEREBY GIVE PERMISSION

for the   Northfield   Cinema,

situate at   Bristol Road South, Northfield

in the said City to be opened and used on Sundays for the purpose of cinematograph entertainments from the first day of January, 1959, until the thirty-first day of December, 1959, subject to the conditions set out below :

1. At all cinemas within approximately half-a-mile radius of Stephenson Place the hours of the entertainment shall be from 3 p.m. to 9.30 p.m.
> (These places include the Odeon, Gaumont, Forum, West End, Scala, Futurist, Gaiety and the two News Theatres.)
> At all other cinemas the hours of the entertainment shall be from 3.30 p.m. to 10 p.m.

2. No person (including the licensee) shall be employed by any employer on any Sunday in connection with a cinematograph entertainment or any other entertainment or exhibition given therewith who has been employed on each of the six previous days either by that employer in any occupation or by any other employer in connection with similar entertainments or exhibitions.

3. The licensee and/or the employer shall keep at the licensed premises a record in an approved form showing the names and addresses *(and in the case of projectionists the ages)* of all persons employed or working on each Sunday, and shall within seven days of receiving a request to that effect from the Clerk to the Justices, produce to him such record for the information of the Justices, together with any copy which may be required. Such records shall at all reasonable times be open to the inspection of the Police and Fire Force Officers and any Inspector of the Justices.

4. Unless the premises are regularly opened for cinematograph exhibitions on Sundays at least seven days' notice in writing shall be given to the Clerk to the Justices of the intention to open the premises on any Sunday. Previous notice shall also be given to him of the closing of any premises regularly opened on Sunday.

5. The licensee, in pursuance of paragraph (*b*) of the proviso to Section 1 (1) of the Sunday Entertainments Act, 1932, shall pay to such persons and in such manner as the Justices may direct, in respect of the period covered by this permission, the sum of £ **132. 0. 0.** , being a sum not exceeding the amount estimated by the Justices as the amount of the profits which will be received from cinematograph entertainments given while the premises are open on Sundays during that period and from any other entertainment or exhibition given therewith, with the intent that the percentage thereof prescribed by the Secretary of State shall be transmitted by the Justices to the Cinematograph Fund constituted in accordance with the Sunday Entertainments Act, 1932, and that the remainder shall be distributed by the Justices to such persons as the Justices may specify for the purpose of being applied to charitable objects.

Provided that if the premises above-mentioned are permanently closed before the thirty-first day of December, 1959, a pro rata reduction shall be allowed in respect of the sum directed to be paid as aforesaid.

6. The conditions attached to the cinematograph licence which are required to be observed on week-days shall be complied with.

7. This permission to open on Sundays is liable to be withdrawn by the Justices in the event of any contravention of the foregoing or any other conditions subject to which the premises are allowed to be opened on Sundays.

GIVEN under the Official Stamp of the Justices, which is hereto affixed under their authority by me.

Clerk to the Justices.

PERMIT: SUNDAY CINEMATOGRAPH ENTERTAINMENTS.

FEE 5/-.

NOTE.—Payment of the amount specified in paragraph 5 is to be made to Mr. R. G. Watchorn, 75, New Street, Birmingham, 2, by four equal quarterly instalments.

100   10/12/58

FRED ASTAIRE — born 10th May 1899 and voted the entertainer of the Century by a National American Magazine, gave us so much pleasure with his dancing, firstly with his Sister, Adele, and then with Ginger Rogers, Rita Hayworth, Eleanor Powell, Vera-Ellen and Cyd Charisse.

A BIRMINGHAM TALKIE.

[Birmingham Justices, at their meeting yesterday, decided in favour of continuing their present policy in regard to Sunday entertainments. An amendment providing for the Sunday opening of cinemas was defeated.]

Ginger Rogers

There was a lot of controversy regarding the opening of Cinemas in Birmingham on Sundays. Mrs W.A. Potts, (one of the founders of the Cinema Inquiry Committee) said, "I think the question of the kind of film to be shown should have been settled first. I am in favour of Sunday opening so long as films that are a credit to the city are shown, but if we are to have the same programmes that are shown for the rest of the week I am afraid that very often it will be undesirable".

Sir Herbert Austin replied, "I think it is a step in the right direction, it can do no harm, and might do a lot of good, especially in the direction of giving young people something better to do than wander aimlessly about the streets. The censor has sufficient powers to prevent anything being shown that is unsuitable for Sunday entertainment, and it cannot be said that Sunday opening will mean many people having to work".

Sir Charles Rafter, Chief Constable of Birmingham stated that he was in support of Sunday cinema opening as a way of keeping young people out of the public houses.

In November 1932 it was decided by the City Justices, when, by a majority they granted the application of the local Cinematograph Exhibitors Association for licences for all cinemas to open on Sundays from 6.00 to 10.30 p.m. for 12 months. A proportion of the Sunday takings had to be given to local charities.

"I remember the Lozells Cinema, Birmingham very well, serials with Ken Maynard, Tim McCoy and other legendary western stars. Buster Crabbe in the early sci-fi epics. Pearl White in her never ending troubles. Perhaps one of the attractions was the wonderful cinema organ that came from the depths to entertain us.

These thoughts prompted me to hearken back to other directions. For instance how many now remember the cinema that stood opposite the Aston Hippodrome on the corner of Newtown Row? To live up to its name, it actually did have a globe (see photograph) over the marble facade.

Then there was the other cinema at the other end of Newtown Row, (see photograph) the Newtown Palace. There was an added attraction in the programme here. Apart from the serial and films, they usually had live acts. These, I recollect, were usually balancing acts, ventriloquists, and once a talking parrot. It was just as well he, the bird, did not use his street vocabulary on stage. He belonged to a newsagents in Farm Street, and when his cage was hung out of the middle window, any taunting by children brought out a sailor's range of words.

The stage and curtains obviously betokened its former existence as a theatre. As children, we often went especially to follow serials.

At the top of Wheeler Street there stood another small cinema, the Great Hampton. The name belied it, as it was such a small place. It was on the corner of Kenyon Street. I remember seeing Marie Dressler and Wallace Berry, a popular but unlikely film team, in "Min and Bill". It was this film's success which led to a number of films with this popular pair. I might add that it did not look like a cinema, rather like one of the many factories that stood around it.

Finally, more towards Snow Hill, there was the Metropole. This was a fascinating building. It was a theatre in its early days. It had, ground floor, boxes, circle and upper circle. To get to the first two one paid in the foyer, but for the upper deck, there was an entrance at the end of the facade. We paid our money and then went up the stairs. It seems as though there were hundreds to small feet. Although it was an effort, it was necessary for if one went downstairs, you never knew what would be dropped down from above.

I think we had many happy hours there. One of the attractions I remember was Marilyn Miller, the early talkie adaptation of the stage hit Sally, or was it Sunny?

Days of long ago but tinged with sadness now they are gone. Life was gentler, less complicated, even if times were hard. Now life has become complicated and harder. Then we even enjoyed the long trudge to these places and got nearly as much pleasure out of that as we did seeing the actual show, and certainly although the standard of the films was sometimes crude and stilted, I prefer them to the blatant efforts of today's offerings. Horror, sex, and the blatant brutality."

E. Wardell.
Kings Heath, Birmingham.

Claude Rains.

Marie Dressler and Wallace Berry
in the 1930's hit film 'Min and Bill'.

Nelson Eddy

The keyboard of a typical cinema organ
that was installed in the major cinemas
in Birmingham in the 30's.

This type of organ was installed
in the Wylde Green Pavilion.

Jack Warner is remembered
for his Dixon of Dock Green
series.

GENERAL INFORMATION

The British Board of Film Censors classifies films for public exhibition into three categories, 'A', 'H' and 'U'. 'A' Certificate denotes that the film may not be seen by children under the age of 16 years unless accompanied by a parent or guardian.

'H' Certificate category allocated to films of a 'Horrific' nature and excluded all children under the age of 16 years.

'U' Certificate category allocated to films indicated that it was suitable for showing universally, including to unaccompanied children.

'A' Picture — A production intended to be booked as the main feature in a cinema programme, thereby being allocated the largest share of the takings.

'B' Picture — A production intended to be booked as the second feature in a cinema programme and consequently budgeted in terms of those market potentialities.

A Feature Film is defined by the Cinematograph Films Act 1938, as 'a film the length of which is not less than 3,000 feet' (33 minutes)

"To anyone who lived in Small Heath in the 1930's—40's the Coventry Road was an absolute mecca for the film goer. I was only a youngster but the cinema going habit started early with the Saturday matinees. Every cinema it seemed had a different atmosphere and a different serial. The Adelphi always seemed to have a good old Western. The manager, I believe was a Mr Crane and there was a nice lady in the cash box who seemed to be always there and ready to take the money from my grubby little fingers. The doorman was rather a different type. He regarded us as little terrors and used to chase up and down the aisles waving a cane if we misbehaved, which we often did I suppose. Later, during the war I remember the Adelphi had a spitfire plane on its front car park — part of its publicity for the film, "A Target for Tonight". I can also recall a visit to see one of the 'Tarzan' films in the early 40's. Unfortunately halfway through the film stopped, the manager came on to the stage and announced that, "The alert had been sounded, if we wished to leave please do so — the show would go on". My Mother, bless her, thought home was the place to be so we left. I never did see the rest of that film!

The Coronet was a good little cinema. You entered the front up a number of white marble steps. If the sun was shining when you came out the reflection almost blinded you. The managers here were a Mr Last and Mr Baker. I used to queue up for the Front Stalls in a little crush hall down Watts Road. The room was divided down the middle with a rail which kept us in some sort of order. One of the treats here was the person with a basket who sold packets of troach drops and other tasty tit-bits. If you got in early before they started the attendant often came round with a large scent spray and filled the theatre with the aroma of flowers, probably to hide the smell of our troach drops, chips and oranges. I clearly remember seeing "Top Hat" at the Coronet when it was first released — great stuff — also "Suez" with Tyrone Power and lots of musicals of Deanna Durbin and Gloria Jean.

I was only about ten I suppose but I was becoming very interested in the magic of what went on in the little room at the back of the cinema where the beam of light came from. I often used to gaze back at the little windows. You could do this easily at the Coronet because the "box" was underneath the balcony.

This brings me to the Grange, a large Super Cinema. Inside the theatre the walls were decorated with coloured murals of eastern scenes of camels and pyramids etc., lots of alabaster of bunches of fruit around the murals on the ceiling. The lights were of heavy stained leaded light chandelier. The windows along the side, also of leaded lights, used to open before the show started, in the afternoon the attendant came along with a handle and cranked away like fury to get them to close on time. Here again we were treated to the lovely scent spray.

The manageress of the Grange — a Miss Simms — was an old school friend of my mother's. Here was a grand chance to see what went on in the "projection box". I looked, I saw and it conquered me, for I landed a part time job as relief projectionist. I became a great friend of the Chief Operator, a Mr Stanley. I was still at Waverley Grammar School at this time but the odd evening, every Sunday and during school holidays saw me at the Grange. There I stayed as relief projectionist for the next seventeen years until it closed in October 1959. Occasionally, with other members of the staff, we used to stand on the flat roof and gaze down at the long queues forming along Grange Road underneath the canopy. This gave you a feeling of importance to think that they were coming to see the results of your work."

Albert Williams

A citizen of Birmingham, Alexander Parkes, of Bath Row, who was an industrial chemist, artist and tube manufacturer did in 1862 invent a material which he named PARKESINE, now known as CELLULOID, from this the art of roller photography was formulated, using this material, which completely revolutionalised the photographic industry. The principle of this system is now well known and was the forerunner of the film used in the motion picture industry today.

Copy of a letter received by Dorothy Dewey in October 1915 from Charles Chaplin, written on the back of the photograph was the words, "Merrily Chas. Chaplin".

CHARLES CHAPLIN — 1889-1978. King of the clowns — born in Walworth, London, his mother was a soubrette on the variety stage and his father a vaudeville artist. His many films included "Monsieur Verdoux", "The Pilgrims", "Shoulder Arms", "The Gold Rush", "City Lights", "The Great Dictator" and "Modern Times". There is a statue erected to his memory in Leicester Square, London, with the inscription, "The Comic genius who gave pleasure to so many".

This type of viewer was given to patrons in the early 1960's.

"My parents and I always went to the cinema on Friday evenings. My mother and myself usually met my father outside the Piccadilly in Stratford Road, Sparkbrook, although we also attended the Carlton, on Taunton Road and the Waldorf, in Walford Road.

A film which particularly left an impression on my youthful mind (I was about eight years old at the time) was H.G. Wells' "The Shape of Things to Come" and I well remember seeing this at the Piccadilly.

The Carlton was bombed in 1941 with a number of people sheltering inside being killed. The film it was showing at the time was "Typhoon" starring Dorothy Lamour. When the cinema was patched up and re-opened, later in the war, by the then Lord Mayor of Birmingham Councillor Walter Lewis, it recommenced by showing "Typhoon" and I was at the opening ceremony.

The Olympia, in Ladypool Road, had an unenviable reputation as a 'flea-pit' and a quick glance through the exit door at once revealed a battered interior, which I found so off-putting, that I never actually crossed the threshold.

The first film which I can recollect seeing was in 1934, at the Hockley Brook Palladium. It was "Sing as we Go", starring Gracie Fields. The second feature was a Laurel and Hardy film, "Babes in Toyland" and my mother allowed me to sit through it twice! Shortly afterwards, we left Hockley and moved to Sparkhill to begin patronising the cinemas I have mentioned.

As I became older, I was allowed to attend the cinema on my own, and as it was necessary for children under sixteen years of age to be accompanied by an adult if a certificate "A" film was showing, I frequently had to wait outside and ask some kindly older person to take me in.

As I approached sixteen, of course, this subterfuge was no longer necessary and I began a spell about 1943 onwards of going to the cinema three times a week. This often necessitated taking in cinemas slightly farther afield, such as the Tyseley in Warwick Road, Greet, where I saw Danny Kaye for the first time in "Up In Arms". At the Warwick, farther along Warwick Road in Acocks Green, I recall seeing the "Phantom of the Opera" starring Claude Rains.

Of course, a number of cinemas in Birmingham were originally Theatres. One such was the Bordesley Palace, another the Gaiety in Coleshill Street, where I saw "Three into Two Won't Go", shortly before it was demolished in 1970 as part of the clearance programme from the University of Aston campus. I was employed at the University at the time, and was told that when a theatre, Charles Chaplin had appeared there with Fred Karno's company prior to going to America in 1910.

My favourite film of my early period (I still remain an enthusiast) was "Death of a Salesman" starring Frederic March. This did not have a wide general release in Birmingham and I had to go to the Stockland at Stockland Green to see it in 1951."

Colin J. Simpson
Solihull

Dulcie Gray

Ramon Novarro

Edward Arnold

Two types of advertisements to be found in trade journals and Year Books in the 1940's.

An outing of cinema managers in the 1920's. Mr H. Dewey, the manager of the Springfield Picture Playhouse at that time, and the inventor of the 'Reflecta Screen' which he patented in 1919 and subsequently installed in over 600 cinemas and theatres in all parts of the country, is seated in the centre of the picture 2nd row 7th from the right.

Gable meets his match in Mabel

AND THE SCREEN BREAKS INTO SONG TO CELEBRATE !!

A HIT...
AS BIG AS THE
STARS IT UNITES!

Marion and Clark, surrounded by the madcap mirth and merry melody that mark Warner Bros. as the master makers of musical hits!

MARION
DAVIES
CLARK
GABLE
in
"CAIN
and
MABEL"
with
ALLEN JENKINS
ROSCOE KARNS
WALTER CATLETT
DAVID CARLYLE-HOBART
CAVANAUGH . Directed
by LLOYD BACON . Music
and Lyrics by Harry
Warren and Al Dubin
A Warner Bros . Picture
A Cosmopolitan Production

CERT. "U"

MAGNIFICENT IN SPECTACLE—

HILARIUS IN COMEDY

THRILLING IN ACTION

AND FULL SUPPORTING PROGRAMME.

Since 1960 the following cinemas, or establishments that give film performances, have been opened and are still operative, they have no nostalgic interest, the one exception being the Odeon Cinema, Birmingham Road, Sutton Coldfield, opened in 1936. As the reader is aware Sutton Coldfield was incorporated into the city of Birmingham in 1975.

Birmingham Queensway
Odeon Film Centre.

Triangle Cinema
Gosta Green.

The Cinema,
Midland Arts Centre,
Cannon Hill Park.

This is the type of advertisement that was displayed in the Local Press by the Cinematograph Exhibitors Association on behalf of its members. This particular one appeared in the Birmingham Mail on the 7th February, 1952.

TWENTY FAMOUS FILMS FROM WHICH YOU MUST SELECT TWELVE.

A—Way Down East.
B—Over the Hill.
C—The Old Nest.
D—Pay Day.
E—The Four Horsemen of the Apocalypse.
F—Orphans of the Storm.
G—My Boy.
H—Queen of Sheba.
I—Squibs Wins the Calcutta Sweep.
J—Peacock Alley.
K—A Yankee at the Court of King Arthur
L—Through the Back Door.
M—Rob Roy.
N—Smilin' Through.
O—The Molly Coddle.
P—The Kid.
Q—Nanook of the North.
R—A Bill of Divorcement.
S—The Great Day.
T—A Sailor-Made Man.

- - - - CUT COUPON NEATLY ROUND THIS LINE - - - - -

My List of the best and most popular twelve films in order of merit is as follows:

1	2	3	4	5	6	7	8	9	10	11	12

(Indicate name of film by the initial letter only, PRINTED IN BLOCK LETTERS. Thus if you consider "Pay Day" the most popular film of all you will place the letter "D" underneath No. 1.)

I enclose P.O. for 1/- and enter this Competition upon and subject to the Conditions published in the "Sunday Pictorial" and agree to abide by such conditions and to accept the decisions of the Adjudicating Committee upon all matters and questions which may arise in connection with this Competition as absolutely final and legally-binding.

NAME ....

ADDRESS ....

SEND IN YOUR VOTE AT ONCE—THIS COUPON WILL BE REPEATED IN NEXT WEEK'S "SUNDAY PICTORIAL."

This competition appeared in the "Sunday Pictorial", April 23rd 1923. 1st Prize £3,000, 2nd £1,500, 3rd £500, plus ten prizes of £100. This typifies the interest in films in the early days.

This hoarding outside the Northfield Cinema was typical of many to be seen on the city cinema sites.

CINEMATOGRAPH EXHIBITORS' ASSOCIATION

Sundays 4—10 p.m. Houses marked * denotes six-day programme.

99

A Weststar Projector with a Peerless Arc Lamp

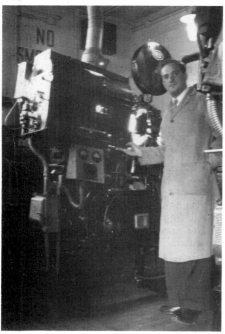

F.A. Williams in the Projection
Room at the Grange Cinema, Small
Heath 1959

A KALEE Projector with a Vulcan Type Arc Lamp
and Western Sound equipment.

A KALEE Regal Arc Lamp

Hazel Court, born 20th February 1926 in Handsworth, Birmingham, attractive red head, started her career at the Birmingham Repertory Theatre. Leading lady in several horror films including "The Mask of Death" with Vincent Price. Resident U.S.A.

Beryl Baxter, born 9th April 1925 in Birmingham, educated in Brighton & Hove, first stage appearance, Shakespeare Memorial Theatre, Stratford-on-Avon, in 1943. First film appearance was in 1947 in the film, "The Idol of Paris".

Pauline Grant, born 29th June 1915 in Moseley, Birmingham, educated St Paul's Convent, Edgbaston, first stage appearance, The People's Theatre, St. Pancras, December 1937. Was director of Ballet at the Neighbourhood Theatre, Kensington in 1940. First film appearance was in 1945 in the film, "Uncut Diamonds".

Raymond Huntley, born 23rd April 1904 in Birmingham, educated at King Edward's School, Birmingham. First stage appearance was at the Birmingham Repertory Theatre in April 1922, appeared in hundreds of productions, made appearances in numerous films from 1934 onwards, including "Rembrandt" "Room at the Top" and "Trio".

Margaret Leighton, born 26th February 1922 in Barnt Green, Worcs., educated Church of England College, Edgbaston, first stage appearance was at the Birmingham Repertory Theatre in September 1938. First appeared in films in 1948 in the film, "Bonnie Prince Charlie" with David Niven and Jack Hawkins.

Alan Napier, born on the 7th January 1903 in Harborne, Birmingham, educated at Packwood Haugh and Clifton College. Studied at the Royal Academy of Dramatic Art, first stage appearance at the Playhouse, Oxford in May 1924. A prolific actor, his film appearances included "Julius Caesar", "Journey to the Centre of the Earth", "In a Monastery Garden" and "Marnie".

Webster Booth, born on the 21st January 1902 in Birmingham, actor and Vocalist, educated at Lincoln Cathedral Choir and Aston Commercial School, made his first appearance on the stage at the Theatre Royal, Brighton. Married Anne Ziegler, they toured the World singing together. Studied singing under Dr Richard Wassell who was choir master at St Martin's Church, Birmingham and conductor of the Birmingham City Police Band. Appeared in films from 1933 last film "Laughing Lady". Broadcast over 1,000 times with his wife Anne.

Anne Heywood, born 1931, (real name Violet Pretty) in Handsworth, Birmingham, educated at Fentham Road Secondary Modern School, Erdington. Cinema usherette and beauty queen. Appeared in numerous films including "90 Degrees in the Shade", "The Chairman" and "The Fox". Resident in Hollywood, U.S.A.

Brian Aherne, born 2nd May 1902 in King's Norton area Worcs., later incorporated into the City of Birmingham. Educated in the Edgbaston Area and later attended Malvern College, made his first stage appearance with the Pilgrim Players, in April 1910 in Birmingham. Commenced his film career in 1924, one of his favourite films was "The Beaux Stratagem". Resident California, U.S.A.

Richard Wordsworth, born 19th January 1915 in Halesowen, Worcs., educated at Loretto and Queen's College, Cambridge, first stage appearance was at the Old Vic Theatre, in London in October 1938. His films include "the Man Who Knew Too Much" and "The Quatermass Experiment" with Brian Donlevy and Jack Warner.

G. Melville Cooper, born in Birmingham 15th October 1896, educated at King Edward's School, Birmingham. His first stage appearance was at Stratford on Avon in 'Return of the Prodigal', he made his film debut in 1934 in the films "The Scarlet Pimpernel" and "Private Life of Don Juan", other films included "Adventures of Robin Hood" and "From the Earth to the Moon", he made numerous Television appearances.

Joyce Barbour, born 27th March 1901 in Birmingham, made her first stage appearance in Birmingham in 1914 as a Fairy in a pantomime, made numerous stage appearances in London from 1917 to 1958, she also appeared in several films.

Hazel Court

Anne Heywood

Brian Aherne

The End

The OAK CINEMA, Bristol Road, Selly Oak, Birmingham,
opened in 1923 closed in 1979, in the process of being
demolished in December 1984

IN CONCLUSION

Cinemas, after all were only buildings made of bricks and mortar and put together by workmen working to the master plan, projected by the Architect using his expert knowledge of design, decor and technique. What gave each cinema its special quality was the manager and his staff of experts, so often taken for granted by the patrons. The Chief projectionist, second projectionist, commissionaires, usherettes, cashier etc., each played their part in giving each cinema its special personality and atmosphere. I wish to thank them, on behalf of all patrons, for their devotion to duty, putting up with long standing unsociable hours, especially for their service to the community during the War years.

Mr B.T.Davis, branch Chairman of the Cinematograph Exhibitors Association, at a meeting held in Birmingham on the 18th January 1946 said, "It had been recorded with pride that not a single cinema in the city had closed down, even during the worst days of the war, unless it was knocked down by enemy action". What a tribute!

I wish to thank the reader of this book for purchasing it and thereby aiding a worthy charity.

VJP

ACKNOWLEDGEMENTS

To Alton Douglas, my nephew, who suggested that I wrote this book and for his guidance and encouragement.
To Chris Bryan, manager of the Warwick Cinema, Acocks Green, for his help, advice and interest.
To the Editors of the Birmingham Post & Mail, Solihull News, Solihull Times, Birmingham Reference Library (Local Studies Dept.), The Birmingham & Midland Institute, The British Film Institute, The City of Birmingham Cinematograph, Licensing & Planning Depts., Candid Camera, Len Baron, L.J. Bather, May Belsten, Doris Brown, M.C. Cameron, C.M. Cheshire, James Cole, John Duddy, L. Dyer, C.A. Edwards, Frank Ellis, N. Fisher, L.A. Gibbons, J. Goddard, Jill Hetzel, R. Huckfield, Alfred Hughes, F.S. Hunt, W.A. James, S.A. Job, Joan N. Jones, Eurwyn Jones, A Judd, A.T. Lee, Ernest Lewis, David Lukeman, J.L. Marks, Stan Mason, Ruby Massa, R.C. Mayfield, Muriel Merchant, W. Morgan, Ena M. Parker, Janet Page, Rose Parkes, R.J. Payton, Henry S. Pinchin, C. Povey, George Pursall, Sheila Rawlins, Leonard Rose, Derek S. Shutts, Colin J. Simpson, Frank Smith, Hazel Smith, Frank Speed, R. Voyce, E. Wardell, Tom Watkins, Albert Williams and my wife Veronica for proof reading the entire book.

The ARCADIAN CINEMA, Ladywell Walk, off Hurst Street near the Birmingham Hippodrome. Opened on the 14th November 1991 by the Lord Mayor of Birmingham, Councillor Bill Turner. General manager Michael Jackson. It has 9 auditoriums. Full details of the opening programmes are on the displayed programme. It cost the MGM £7 million. It is now the main cinema for Birmingham residents. Tel No. 0121 622 5551

The ODEON QUEENSWAY, Smallbrook Queensway. This opened on 8th March 1970 but it closed on the 18th September 1988. The COMPTON CINEMA was originally on this site and opened in the 1960's as a private cinema. It was later enlarged and re-built and then called the SCALA SUPERAMA CINEMA. It had a Grand Civic opening by the Lord Mayor on the 23rd November 1964. It has a seating capacity of 604. It was taken over by the ODEON in 1970.

SHOWCASES CINEMAS BIRMINGHAM, Kingstanding Road, Erdington. This opened on the 7th August 1992 and has 12 screens and a seating capacity for 3500.

The TRIANGLE CINEMA, Holt Street, Gosta Green. This opened on the 25th August 1977. It was then called the Art Lab Cinema. It has a seating capacity for 177. It closed on the 31st July 1994 showing the film 'Jesus of Montreal'.

The MAC CINEMA, Cannon Hill Park. This opened on the 19th October 1987 and was under the management of Robert Petty. It has a seating capacity for 144.